D1551349

MY FAMILY
TELLS
THIS STORY

Snow Flower

HERITAGE BOOKS, INC.

Published 1999 by

HERITAGE BOOKS, INC.
1540-E Pointer Ridge Place
Bowie, Maryland 20716
1-800-398-7709

www.heritagebooks.com

ISBN 0-7884-1136-5

A Complete Catalog Listing Hundreds of Titles
On Genealogy, History, and Americana
Available Free Upon Request

DEDICATION

After the Creator and my Ancestors, there are two very special people
who deserve as much credit for this book as I.

First, my husband Dale, who puts up with the cemetery walks,
takes many photos for me, and listens patiently for hours as I run on
about my favorite subject.

Secondly, my sister Mato Woksapa Winan, who is constantly handing
me a book and saying "Oh, you just have to read this one. Just one
more." "Just one more" has turned into many, but her input and
encouragement have been invaluable.

CONTENTS

THANK YOUS

There have been many others who have shared information with me. I owe each a vote of thanks, and I could never have put all of this together without them. They are:

Laurie Beth Duffy, editor of *Native American Ancestry Hunting*. Her advice and input have meant more to me than I can ever say.

Richard Pangburn, author of *The Indian Blood* series, who heard me speak and recommended me to Laurie Beth.

Vila Curry, whose constant input is both refreshing and heartening.

Steven Heisey, who often calls with new information.

Jerry Ward, who never fails to encourage.

Wantangasa, who allowed me the use of her "Red Flags" paper.

James Fredenburgh, who sees that I have copies of Indian newspapers.

SEARCHING FOR FIRST AMERICAN ANCESTRY

There are several things that we must understand before we begin to look at our family history.

For instance, how is it that First American people came to have European sounding names?

There were two groups of people who protected and cared for the Native. These groups taught them how to look and act as "whites," giving them jobs and supporting them during the learning period. These people were the English Quakers and the German Amish. When you are forced to protect yourself and your family by assuming a new identity, you do this by taking the names of people you know well, those who have helped you and those you most admire. This is the reason that so many of our people have German and English sounding names. Then, too, many just kept the names given them by the German and English speakers who dubbed them "Billy" or "Joe." When the name is not really yours, one works as well as another.

Because it was the Amish and the Quakers who helped and protected our people, you will also be looking for those who have lived for a time in an area known to be Amish or Quaker, but who do not profess either religion. For instance, I have an ancestor who lived in a Quaker area long enough to have a child, then moved to the Black Swamp area of northern Ohio. A friend has an ancestor who was a doctor in an Amish town. In neither case is there any record or history of the person being of that faith.

This search will not be easy, for after 1830 it was illegal to be "Indian" and live east of the Mississippi River. The federal government had passed the Removal Act, which called for the removal of all First American people to land west of the Mississippi. If you were caught living as First American people in the east, your property could be confiscated and you and your family would be shipped west to one of the concentration camps known as reservations. Those of our ancestors who could pass as "white" people pretended that is what they were. Those who did not have light skin claimed to be "black." In either case, they gave up the old religions, or went underground with them; gave up the old ways of living, or stated that this was the way it was done in "the old country." They lost much of their tribal background, even ties to family who had gone west.

If you were willing, you could sign a pledge to the United States, saying that you gave up your Indian rights and wanted to be considered a U.S. citizen. Many people did this. That is the reason so many western people will argue that everyone went west. If you gave up your heritage, they no longer considered you a part of the tribe.

The First American form of adoption, whether the person be a "white" captive, a child from another family (although children were thought to belong to the entire tribe, so an adoption would not take place within the tribe, unless for a very special reason), or a captive from another tribe, would have been to wash the adoptees in the river, give them new clothes which were specially made for them (or, in some cases, for the person they were replacing), and then never to consider that they had ever been other than the persons they became upon the adoption.

The process works both ways. First American people could un-adopt their own people, who would sign over their "Indian" rights and agree to be "white" so that they could stay behind and not face removal.

As one person I was working with said, "I can't help what my ancestors did. I want my heritage back. I am not the one who signed it away." I agree with this, and in the course of doing what I do, I have met countless others who feel the same.

Because of these things, you will be unlikely to find any record which states that the person you are researching is "Indian." Instead, you will look carefully at your family for certain signs that are clues to First American people in hiding.

Those are the things that I am going to try to help you understand.

Once your search is finished, you will establish that you do have First American ancestry by a process called triangulation. You will place the name in an area that can be identified as Native and do it at a time when you can show a certain tribe was in that area.

So, let us begin:

Indian ancestry stories were carefully passed from one generation to another with the admonition not to tell. Only quiet, closed-mouthed children were told. They, in turn, passed the story to the next generation in the same way. This practice explains why often only one side of a family knows the history.

If your family tells such a story, go to the oldest living relative who will discuss it. Many will not; they remember the admonition. Ask your relative to write the story down just as he or she remembers it, sign it, date it, and have it notarized. Keep this paper with your genealogy. It will become one of your most important papers. This is proof of the story and the fact that the family always knew of the First American ancestry.

Next, go to your friendly neighborhood library or genealogy society and purchase two forms, one called a Pedigree Chart and one called a Family Group Sheet. I have shown you examples in the next few pages. Not all are exactly like this, there are minor differences, but the process is the same, and that is what matters.

Then photocopy them, and keep blank forms as master copies. You will need more Family Group Sheets than Pedigree Charts, but we will get into that later.

Next, take a Pedigree Chart and put yourself on line number one. The sheet will lead you from there, if you will allow it to. Your father goes on line number two and your mother on three. Proceed in this manner as far as you can go. Enlist the aid of your family to help you. Fill in as much about each person as you can. If you reach the end of a section (later, we will be referring to these as family lines), begin another page by taking the last person and making him or her number one on the new page. Again, go as far as you can. When you reach the point where you can go no further, you will know where you need to start looking. I like

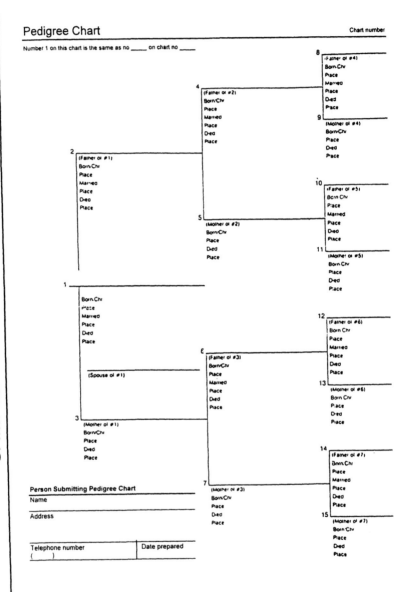

Family Group Record

Page ___ of ___

Husband's name		
Born	Place	
Chr.	Place	
Mar.	Place	
Died	Place	
Bur.	Place	
Father		Mother
Husband's other wives		

Wife's name		
Born	Place	
Chr.	Place	
Mar.	Place	
Died	Place	
Bur.	Place	
Father		Mother
Wife's other husbands		

Children List each child (whether living or dead) in order of birth

1 Sex	Name		Spouse
	Born	Place	
	Chr.	Place	
	Mar.	Place	
	Died	Place	
2 Sex	Name		Spouse
	Born	Place	
	Chr.	Place	
	Mar.	Place	
	Died	Place	
3 Sex	Name		Spouse
	Born	Place	
	Chr.	Place	
	Mar.	Place	
	Died	Place	
4 Sex	Name		Spouse
	Born	Place	
	Chr.	Place	
	Mar.	Place	
	Died	Place	

☐ Check here if additional children are listed on another Family Group Records, and attach the record to this form. Include parents' names.

Additional Information

SAMPLE • FAMILY GROUP RECORD

to concentrate on one person at a time, and not go any further until I am
certain that I have gleaned all the information that I can on that person.

But, before you begin the search, make a Family Group Sheet for each
male on your Pedigree Chart. You will pick up the women as you go.
Again, fill in as much information as you can. List all children. If one
sheet will not do, use as many as you need to complete a family. I have
one ancestor with two marriages and twenty-eight children. It took eight
sheets to complete that family.

I like to take a highlighter and highlight my direct ancestor. That way,
when I flip to that page, I know at a glance who I am looking at.

If an ancestor has been married more than once and had children by
other mates, list them as a separate family unit behind the family your
ancestor belonged in. Sometimes, it is necessary to trace an ancestor
through a sibling, so you need to know as many brothers and sisters as
possible.

Now, begin with the family known to have First American ancestry.
Who is that ancestor? How close are you to him or her?

I believe that the best way to help you may be to describe my searches
for you.

My family story said that my grandfather's grandmother had an Indian
name that translated to Snow Flower; that she belonged to a tribe which
traveled Indiana, Ohio, and Kentucky; and that she was Tecumseh's
niece.

Now, flipping over into First American ancestry: each person belongs to
a Clan. The members of your Clan are your family. They will be your
brothers, sisters, aunts, uncles, nieces, or nephews. So, being
Tecumseh's niece does not mean that she is of the same blood family; it
means, instead, that she is Shawnee Water Panther Clan, because that
was Tecumseh's Clan. In coming to understand this much, I was far
ahead of many people with stories, because I knew at the beginning that
I was looking for Shawnee ancestry. There were family stories which
said that she was Cherokee, among others, so I did check them all out,
just to be certain.

I did not know who my great-grandmother was. I only knew she was Mary Jane, that her mother had died when she was four, that she had been in an orphanage in St. Mary's, Ohio, that her last name had been Rager, and that her first husband was named Miller. My grandfather was the oldest child by her second husband, Alveso Needles.

My family is historically from Licking County, Ohio, and my grandmother had gone to great lengths to tell me about my family there. Again, I had a head start over most of you, because I knew a lot of my ancestry as a child. However, I could not find my grandfather as a child in Licking County. Finally, I got the bright idea of getting a look at his death certificate. These can be found at county health departments. After fifty to seventy-five years, at least in Ohio, most can be found at the state historical society library. What a surprise to find that Grandpa was born in Clark County, Ohio! I would have never guessed.

His death certificate also told me his birth and death dates, how he died, where he lived, where he is buried, how old he was, who his wife was, and who his doctor and the undertaker were. It also named his parents. Of course, I knew most of this; I am pointing it out to you so that you see what a valuable source of information these records can be.

Now the search was on for his mother, who is the daughter of Snow Flower. She is buried in the same cemetery as Grandpa, so I knew her death date. I also now knew that she had lived in Enon, Clark County, Ohio. But, from my father, I found that she was living with my grandparents when she died in Gahanna, Franklin County, Ohio. A search of death records at the historical society showed that her name was Mary Jane Rager, that she was born in Gettysburg, Darke County, Ohio, that her father was Michael Rager and her mother was "Susie."

The more family members that you can enlist to help you search, the better. Next in my own search, a niece came up with the marriage record for Michael Rager and Susannah Wagaman in Darke County, Ohio, on April 26, 1854. The 1860 census showed Michael Rager as head of household with a wife named Susie and three children: John who is six, Mary Jane who is four, and William who is two.

DEATH CERTIFICATE • HARRY G. NEEDLES

DIVISION OF VITAL STATISTICS
CERTIFICATE OF DEATH

Pri. Dist. No. 4500   State File No. ____ Registrar's No. 16

PLACE OF DEATH		2. USUAL RESIDENCE
a. COUNTY Licking		a. STATE Ohio b. COUNTY Licking
b. CITY write RURAL... Rural-Monroe Twp.	c. LENGTH OF STAY 8 yrs.	c. CITY write RURAL... Rural-Monroe Twp.
d. FULL NAME OF HOSPITAL OR INSTITUTION Jersey Rd. near Johnstown		d. STREET ADDRESS Jersey Rd. near Johnstown

3. NAME OF DECEASED — a. (First) Harry   b. (Middle) G.   c. (Last) Needles   4. DATE OF DEATH (Month) Jan. (Day) 24, (Year) 1954

5. SEX Male   6. COLOR OR RACE White   7. MARRIED... Married   8. DATE OF BIRTH Aug. 24, 1885   9. AGE 68

10a. USUAL OCCUPATION Retired Caretaker   10b. KIND OF BUSINESS Rocky Fork County Club   11. BIRTHPLACE Enon, Clark Co., Ohio   12. CITIZEN OF WHAT COUNTRY? USA

13. FATHER'S NAME Alveso V. Needles   14. MOTHER'S MAIDEN NAME Mary Rager

WAS DECEASED EVER IN U.S. ARMED FORCES? No   16. SOCIAL SECURITY NO. 288-03-9358   17. INFORMANT'S SIGNATURE Ethel Needles

MEDICAL CERTIFICATION
DISEASE OR CONDITION DIRECTLY LEADING TO DEATH (a) Coronary Occlusion
ANTECEDENT CAUSES Morbid conditions... DUE TO (b) Arteriosclerostic Heart Disease
Pleural Effusion DUE TO (c) Cardiac Decompensation
II. OTHER SIGNIFICANT CONDITIONS

20. AUTOPSY? Yes ☐ No ☐

I hereby certify that I attended the deceased from June 8, 1953, to 1-24-, 1954, and that death occurred at 11:15 A.m., from the causes and on the date stated above.
SIGNATURE Leonard D. Parfitt   (Degree or title) D. O.   23b. ADDRESS Johnstown, Ohio   23c. DATE SIGNED 1-25-54

BURIAL DATE 1-27-54   24c. NAME OF CEMETERY Green Hill Cemetery   LOCATION Johnstown, Ohio

1-27-54 Lloyd J. Crouse   NAME OF EMBALMER L. P. Crouse   (LIC. NO.) 5216 A
Sub-Registrar's Signature

REC'D BY LOCAL 1-27-54   REGISTRAR'S SIGNATURE Mary Lou Hankinson   25. FUNERAL DIRECTOR'S SIGNATURE L. L. Crouse   (LIC. NO.) 2942

I hereby certify that this is a true copy of the **death certificate** on file at the Licking County Health Department.

Mary E. Tomlinson
Registrar - District 4500

The other story about Snow Flower/Susannah Wagaman is that she died in 1861 when her daughter was four and that Michael "was gone" when this happened. We will discuss Michael later. For now, I have my Indian lady with an American identity.

Sometimes very strange, funny and wonderful things happen when you are doing this type of search. On a whim, one Sunday afternoon, my husband and I rode to Greenville, the county seat of Darke County. I wanted to find an address for the genealogy society or the historical society (very often these will be connected) so that I could write and inquire about the Wagaman family.

We found a very large museum which is open on Sundays and features two very famous people from Darke County: Annie Oakley and Lowell Thomas. I have always been a history freak, so you know I would not miss a chance to see a museum. In we went. In the second room I entered, I saw a painting by Martin Wagaman. Well, I must say, I fully intended to check on this man. In the next room, I found several more. I made a bee-line for the office, caught a lady who I later found was the curator, Miss Tony (who must have thought she had a totally crazy woman on her hands), and asked her to tell me all she knew about Martin Wagaman. She had known him personally and he had died in the '60s. Next Question: "Are there any Wagamans left? Do you know of any Wagaman descendant still in this area?" She just stared at me (another reason to believe she thought I was nuts). I said, "My great-great-grandmother was Susannah Wagaman from Gettysburg."

Then she asked me if there were any Millers involved. I said, "Yes, the daughter married a Miller." She picked up the telephone, dialed a number, and said, "Nancy, there is a lady standing in my office that you really need to talk to."

Well ...... Nancy and I talked until they closed the museum. We compared family notes and, yes, we really were related. Then I asked the big question, "What do you know about the Indian ancestry in the Wagaman family?"

She said, "There is none."

My reply, "That's not what MY family says."

The only known photo of Susannah Wagaman Rager (aka Snow Flower) appears to have been taken shortly before her death in 1861. The original photo shows the side of a hide-covered structure. Notice that she is wearing a pouch which is covered in the same material as her dress. Her braids appear to be tied with leather thongs. You will want to watch your family photos for unusual items of dress. I have a friend whose great-grandmother is wearing some very strange-looking footwear in a photo; these turned out to be crow boot-style moccasins. Another friend brought me a photo of her great-grandmother, who is wearing a nose ring! It is the only time that I have ever seen a woman wear a nose ring. A very telling photo.

We argued for several months, and one day I received a telephone call: "I think I owe you an apology. I was walking out of the museum with an older lady who is a member of the Wagaman family, when I mentioned that I was going to go over the family one more time. She turned to me and said, 'Well, you do know they are Indian, don't you?'"

YES! Vindication. If you feel the story is right and that you are on the right track, do not be deterred by skeptics.

Nan, the skeptical lady I told you about earlier, was able to give me the rest on this family. Susannah was the daughter of Jacob Wagaman, who was born in Montgomery County, Ohio, in 1810, and Mary (Polly) Overly.

Jacob's father was Christian Wagaman. The family goes back to Berks County, Pennsylvania.

To the best of my knowledge, no one has been able to find the father of Christian Wagaman. I suspect that we never will. If Jacob was born in 1810, his father would have probably been born around 1770-90, which puts him in the right era and area to be the son of a Delaware Chieftain named Wangoman, who disagreed with Zeisberger (a Moravian missionary and noted First American historian).

The closeness of the names leads me to believe that this is our ancestor. The information on Wangoman comes from Randall and Ryan's *History Of Ohio*.

Richard Pangburn, in *Indian Blood II*, gives a very convincing argument that the Wagamans are Delaware, through a man called Wingenund. Either scenario fits.

Now, let's look at Mary Overly. Nan supplied me with a lineage showing the Overly family back to Germany.

Let me pause here to caution you. If you can find these records, be absolutely certain that this is your family. Then double check everything you see there. Never take anything for granted, or leave any decision to chance.

Mary's father, Martin Overly II, was born in Lancaster County, Pennsylvania, in 1767. Ah — Amish country. No indication that anyone in this family was Amish.

Later, Nan turned up the death certificate of Mary (Polly) Wagaman. It does not give her parents' names, although the form asked for them. What it does show, however, is that she was born in Chillicothe, Ross County, Ohio, BEFORE Chillicothe became a "white" town!

Here is my triangulation. Name, time frame, area.

My "Indian" ancestor appears to have been the product of a Shawnee mother and a Delaware father.

I would like to postulate that Martin Overly in Ross County, Ohio, might have been a case of a First American person "taking" the name of someone who had helped him, perhaps in Lancaster or Berks County, Pennsylvania.

There is also the possibility that there never was a Martin Overly there, since Polly's death certificate does not give her parents' names. There is, however, an Overly Chapel and cemetery. This chapel and cemetery are very interesting, situated on a hill (with the chapel at the bottom) with Native gravestone symbols.

• Another clue for you: small non-denominational chapels. First American people began to use small chapel-like buildings for places of worship when it was no longer possible to worship in the old ways.

• The next thing that I have to tell you is that once you are successful in one line, check the marriages. In nearly every Pedigree Chart that I have seen, the rule seems to hold that where you have one First American ancestor, there will be others.

So, now, let's go back to Michael Rager, Snow Flower's husband.

The family has always claimed that he was German. I have never quite believed it.

Prob. 838-P

Barrett Bross, Publishers, Springfield, Ohio

Certified Copy of Death Record

The State of Ohio, ...AUGLAIZE............County.

Date of Record. . . . May 19, 1873 . . . A. D. 19

No. . 34 . . . . .

Name in full . . . . Polly Wagerman

Date of Death-- Year 1 872 Month . . . . Dec. . . . . Day 15

Condition - (Married, Single or Widowed), ... --

Age—Years. . 74 , Months . . . . -- . . . . . . Days . . . . --

Place of Death. . . Ohio . . Auglaize . . . . Noble

Place of Birth . . Chilocothe

Occupation . . . . --

Name of Parents (when infant without name):

Father . . . not listed

Mother . . . not listed

Color . . . W.

Cause of Death . . . Indirect

Last Place of Residence . . . Noble Tp.

The State of Ohio, . . . Auglaize . . . County.

I, the undersigned, certify that I am Judge of the Court of Common Pleas, Probate Division, within and for said County, which is a Court of Record; that I am ex-officio Clerk of said Court, and by law the custodian of the records and papers required by law to be kept in said Court; and that among others a Record of Deaths was heretofore required by law to be kept therein; and that the foregoing is a true and correct transcript from said record of Deaths, Vol. 1 Page 37 now in this office.

Witness my signature and the seal of said Court,

at . . . Wapakoneta . . . Ohio, this . . . 9th

day of . . . June . . . 19 94

Mark E. _____
Judge

By Wanda M. _____
Deputy Clerk

Look at these facts. There are no photos of the man. No one has ever seen his face. He left his dying wife and their children and was never seen again. Why? At no time, even in the stories told by his daughter, Mary Jane, has there ever been the slightest hint of the animosity typical when there is unrest or anger in a household. There does not seem to have been anything but love between the parents. Why, then, would he leave his wife to die alone, and his children to go to an orphanage?

After the photo of Snow Flower surfaced, it became evident that she was living Native. As a matter of fact, I have been asked what reservation she was on. Yet the woman never left Darke County, Ohio, at a time when it was illegal to be Indian there. I do not believe that any "white" man would take the chance of losing everything to live a Native life, and so I argue that Michael was also Native and left in order to protect the children and keep them from being sent to a reservation. If one of your parents was "white," or you had a "white" sponsor, you could stay behind. Susannah's parents Jacob and Polly had obviously established themselves as "white" in Auglaize County. They took the children. It was when Polly died that they went to the orphanage.

• Next rule. Watch all of your family photos for pictures of people who look like published photos of First American people. My argument about Michael Rager was confirmed almost by accident. One day, as I was searching through Wyandot records, I picked up a copy of Thelma Marsh's *Moccasin Trials To The Cross*.

How astonished I was to turn to page 14 and see the face of my great aunt, Michael Rager's granddaughter, staring at me. The unidentified lady is not, of course, my aunt, but she could well be her twin. As I looked at other photos in Mrs. Marsh's books, I found the face of my grandfather in Chief Monecue, and Michael's son John Rager in Matthew Mudeater.

I copied these faces, just as you see them here, and sent them to Chief Leonard Bearskin who referred me to the person he considered to be the leading authority on the Wyandot people, after the death of Mrs. Marsh. Several letters later, Mr. Aubury Buser told me that he believes Michael's ancestor to be a man named Racer who signed the second Greenville Treaty.

For me, that is proof enough. I consider that Mary Jane Rager was full-blooded First American, making my grandfather, at this point, one half.

But — wait — now we have to consider the stories from the other side of this family.

My great-uncle Homer Needles told his granddaughter that he could remember his "Indian" grandmother living with them when he was twelve. Ah, but Snow Flower died when her daughter was four. Does this mean that the other grandmother, Sarah Noras Butt, was also Native?

Photo above, left, is my grandfather and his three sisters. Superimposed over the top is a photo from *Moccasin Trails to the Cross* by Thelma Marsh.   Notice the resemblance of the superimposed image to the lady on the right, my great aunt Hattie. Photo below, left, is a younger photo of my grandfather with Chief Monacue of the Wyandot. Photo above, right, is Mathew Mudeater, a Wyandot chief.   Photo below, right, is my father's uncle John Rager. These are the son and the grandchildren of Michael Rager. You will need to watch your photos for such resemblances.

• Well, now comes the admonition to walk the cemeteries, if possible. I will digress here, and tell you what to look for.

The Overly Chapel. Note that there is no denomination listed anywhere. This is typical of hidden First American Council Houses.

Note the cemetery on the hillside above the church. First American peoples buried high on the hillsides whenever possible. This cemetery does have First American markings on some of the remaining tombstones.

Note the sign on the second church simply says "Church by Jesus Christ."

The willow tree was the Iroquois tree of life. Before the "white" invasion, willow trees were planted on Iroquois graves. When this could no longer be done, they began to incise them into the gravestones. Willow trees on a headstone will usually indicate an Iroquois burial, Wyandot, Cherokee, etc.

Oak trees, oak leaves, and/or acorns indicate Algonquian people. Shawnee, Ottawa, Miami, etc.

It has been suggested that a ½ or bent over willow could mean a ½ breed. In light of the above information, I should think it very likely.

What appear to be grape leaves may indicate chokecherry. These, along with the maple tree and/or leaf are associated with the Mohawk.

The hand with the finger pointing to heaven. If what you see is the back of the hand, the person is First American. In my experience, most often, this type of marking will indicate Shawnee. If the fingers appear, the person is usually "white."

Clasped hands stand for the first treaty that the Delaware people signed with the "whites." These will, of course, denote a Delaware grave.

A rising sun design could also be taken for a headdress. I have no indication as to tribe, but this design bears watching.

Circles are very important in First American life. Watch carefully any ancestor whose headstone shows anything in a circle.

Watch for obvious clan symbols. Things that are obviously First American: Feathers, Spirit Wheels, etc.

As you walk in the cemeteries, look for obvious mounds. The people buried on top of these formations will probably be First American.

Watch for old sections where trees are interspersed among the gravestones, especially cedar, oak, willow, and maple.

Old eight-sided walled cemeteries. These are usually found in southern Ohio. People buried in eight-sided walled cemeteries will most likely be Telegwa Shawnee.

Something that resembles a daisy, yet doesn't quite. Will usually indicate that the person was a medicine person.

OK, now let us consider Sara Noras Butt. Born in 1838, this daughter of John Butt and Sarah Huston took her first breath in Lancaster County, Pennsylvania. Remember — Amish Country? Again, no Amish connection appears.

The important thing about Lancaster County, Pennsylvania, to most First American families is that it is in the Wyoming Valley. Wyoming Valley was Shawnee country before it became Amish. There was a massacre of Shawnee people in this valley in the late 1700s. Remember, in the beginning I told you that the Amish protected the Natives? I have seen countless Shawnee genealogies with ancestors from Lancaster and surrounding counties.

As happens with so many Native people, John Butt, like Michael Rager, is a dead end. There does not seem to be any information about him. He was raised by an uncle and no one has found who his father was.

So, now we have great-great-grandmothers on both sides as probably Shawnee. The son of Sara Noras Butt and Robert Needles is the man who married Snow Flower's daughter, who has been established as Shawnee and Wyandot. Do you begin to see how this works? These are my grandfather's parents, so now it looks as though Grandpa is three-quarters Native.

OK, now we need to check out his Needles grandparents. Alveso's father is Robert, the son of Archibald and Nancy Kile Needels. Note the spelling change? There is an interesting reason for it. When I was thirteen, I decided to work in the school cafeteria. The lady I usually worked with was Mrs. Flossie Needels.

I come from a very small town. There were forty people in my class. Here is another interesting point, and one you need to look for: small towns where everyone is related. Of the forty people in my class, I was related to thirty. Eight were bused in from another town, and two were sons of ministers in the churches.

I have always been a very curious person, and so one day I asked Mrs. Needels if she did not find it strange that in this little town there were the two families, Needles and Needels, who were not related. Did she think it was possible that, in fact, we were related? I got a very huffy, "Certainly not. No, we are definitely not related."

Never one to take "no" for an answer, I asked my father that evening. He told me that Archibald Needels had married a "typical frontier woman" and had fourteen children. This woman was Nancy Kile. After Nancy's death, Archibald began to court a "very proper" English lady who frowned on his "frontier children." So, when Archibald married this woman, the "frontier children" disowned him by changing the spelling of the name and stating that they were not related, but that, yes, in fact, we were.

Of course, I couldn't wait to get back to the cafeteria to tell Mrs. Needels. When I did so, she turned to me with her hands on her hips and said, "Well, you belong to the side of the family with the 'Indian' heritage and we don't want any part of that." So — watch those "typical frontier women." Could it be that they were all First American?

When I confronted Dad with this, his answer was, "Well, what does it matter? It's too far back to count, anyway."

So, here we have another "Indian" ancestor. Interesting. Nancy Kile Needels did turn out to be Shawnee.

Now we are left with Archibald. Of course, after Dad's story, we know this man is "white." Right? Well......

• There are two books written about the Needels/Needles family. Here is another helper for you. In many county and state libraries, you will find a section for genealogies. These shelves will often contain books that family members have put together showing family roots.

I have been very lucky; I have found five such books on four lines. It never hurts to look. I always ask, whenever I am in an area where I know my family was.

• Also, in most states there was a company which published histories of counties there. In the back of those county histories, you will find vignettes about various families who lived in the area. These vignettes are believable because the families wrote them. There were salesmen who went door to door and sold space in each book. In one such, I found a vignette of Archibald which told about both marriages and named all twenty-eight of his children, both wives, their parents, his parents, as well as where they were born.

Both books on the Needels/Needles line state that John Needels, Archibald's father, was born in Sussex County, Delaware, in 1779. At that time, Sussex County was Nanticoke. There was an English ancestor in 1680, a Quaker woman who was married on the Piankatunk River in Virginia, to a man no one has been able to prove came from anywhere else. So, I believe that John was probably Powhatan and Nanticoke.

He is the great-grandson of the English woman. Let's look at this more closely. If Elizabeth Man did, in fact, marry a Powhatan man, her son William would be one-half Native. William was married in Sussex County, Delaware. If his wife was Nanticoke, then their son would be three-quarters: he would get one-half from his mother and one-quarter from his father.

Thomas, who is the son of that marriage, marries in Sussex County, Delaware. John, Thomas' son, then becomes basically full-blood, again. He gets one-half from his mother, and nearly one-half from his father.

Now, John marries in Louisville, Kentucky, in 1797 and lives in Indiana in an area known to be Shawnee. Ohio was opened for "white" settlement in 1797. Indiana has no "white" people, only trappers and traders. There is a small chance that I am wrong. John could have been a trader, but I have grave doubts about that. So, I believe that John was Powhatan and Nanticoke.

John claimed to be Welsh, which tells me that he spoke with a slight accent. He was also known as "Old Black John."

His wife, Sarah Campbell, is another dead end. To date, we have found nothing to tell us who she was. I have to draw the conclusion that good old Archibald (the son of this union) who married the "very proper English lady" wasn't telling anyone about his heritage.

I recently discovered that the Campbells come from Berkeley County, Virginia, an area we are about to discuss.

When you put this all together and follow it down, my grandfather, who started out as one-quarter Native, is now full-blood.

• You must play detective. Never let go of a theory until you have definitely been proven wrong.

Since I have mentioned books about the family, let me caution you that once you have found such a book, place your family in it, and then read everything. Oh, yes, they can become very boring. But they are also jam-packed full of information.

I have one such book on my grandmother's family. It is called *The Green Tree* and was written by Robert Green, who is a descendant of the third family to settle in Monroe Township, Licking County, Ohio.

In the beginning, Robert states that he knows there is Indian blood in the Green family, but no one has ever been able to identify it.

I believe he has done so without realizing it.

• On page 343, Robert tells the story of Diadema and George Washington Green. Another clue for you. Watch for famous "white" names with something added. Especially in the period from around 1820 to the start of the Civil War, 1860.

Think about this scenario: You know the Removal Act is coming. You do not plan to go. You are trying to establish a "white" identity, and especially want to protect your children. Name your child for a famous "white" person. People will think you so admired that person that you named your child for him. "White" person — "white" child.

I have seen such names as George Washington Green, Isaac Newton Ward, Andrew Jackson Matheney in these genealogies. In the case of women, watch for names like America, Virginia, and there seem to be lots of Marys.

Back to George, who purchased the land containing the Wyandot village of Raccoontown. He took his wife to Raccoontown and left her, while he went back to what became Lancaster, Ohio, to harvest wheat. He was gone for three weeks. During that time, Diadema was told repeatedly, by three Wyandot men, that they were going to kill her husband when he returned. They did not want any "white" men in their town. Then George came home. They took one look at him and said, "Oh, no. Indian no kill white man. Indian white man's friend."

Let's take a close look at that story. It is 1807. Central Ohio. A "white" woman in an Indian town? And she survived? Furthermore, they told this "white" woman that they didn't want any "white" men in their town? The wife of the "white" man who owns the ground under their town? They intend to kill him for the color of his skin, then change their minds when they see him? Does any of this sound strange to you? It certainly does to me.

I do not believe that either person was "white." And I do think we know where the Indian in the Green line is.

Just as a little added information, Randall and Ryan's *History Of The State Of Ohio* says that Chief Tarhe moved his town to what later became Lancaster, Ohio, in 1796. This family arrived there in 1798.

Just the other day I received a letter from Robert, who tells me that he has recently spoken with a member of this family who asked if he could tell her which Indian Tribe Diadema belonged to. Well, finally, someone who knows the Willison family was Native. Diadema was a Willison before her marriage.

Bob went on to tell me that the Willisons lived in Cumberland, Maryland. Cumberland was a Shawnee town.

Another part of *The Green Tree* describes a hog skinning done by early members of the Williamson family. After this is over, someone states that "in the old days, we did not have kettles, so we dug a hole and lined it with bark. We built a large fire into which we placed stones. When the stones were hot, we put them in the water surrounding the hog to make it boil." Red flags flashed all over the place for me. This is not a "white" thing. This is the way First American people cooked until the "white " man taught them how to use kettles!

• I descend from George's brother, Regnald. Something else to watch. Strange spellings. If you do not speak English well, you may not write it at all, or very little. We think Regnald is meant to be Reginald.

This line is very interesting, so I believe that I will go into it for you. I do hope that I am not boring you, but it really is the only way I know to show you what to look for.

• My Grandmother Needles is the Green descendant. Sometimes things that seem unusual can be hints to a person's thinking and background.

When I was fourteen or fifteen, I spent part of one summer with Grandma. I remember, one day she went out to garden. She put on an old housedress, cotton stockings, what I have always thought of as "old lady's shoes" (did your grandmother wear those old black tie-up shoes?), a man's flannel work shirt, gloves, and a large brimmed straw hat. I need to add that the flannel shirt was buttoned up all the way.

I said, "Grandma, it's 90 degrees outside! You will suffocate in that getup!"

She stared at me and finally said, "Well, I wouldn't want anyone to think I was Indian."

It wasn't until many years later that I began to believe she may well have been.

The Green family came with a large group of others from Berkeley County, Virginia, now West Virginia. They came first to what later became Lancaster, Ohio. Remember Tarhe's town? They then moved in mass, so to speak, to what was to become Johnstown, Licking County, Ohio. Just outside of Johnstown is the site of Raccoontown. To this day, if you travel to Upper Sandusky, the site of the Wyandot Reservation in Ohio, and tell them you are from Johnstown, they will nod and say, "Oh, Raccoontown."

The history books say that the First Americans left Raccoontown in 1807, but I have seen a postcard with a photo of "The Indian village at Johnstown" dated 1921.

• Something else you should always do: when you discover where your family came from, find out as much as you can about that area. History books say that Berkeley County was Tuscaroras, but there was a Shawnee settlement on the Opecan Creek.

The Shawnee by Jerry E. Clark states that there were Shawnee settlements in Shenandoah County, Virginia, and Oldtown, Maryland, one of them well into the eighteenth century. This is the correct area for the Green family before they came to Ohio.

The History of the Lower Shenandoah Valley Counties of Frederick, Berkeley, Jefferson and Clarke, edited by J. E. Norris and published by

A. Warner and Company, puts the Delaware and the Tuscaroras in Berkeley.

So, I thought these people were most likely Tuscaroras, but some new evidence says that Blue Jacket came from this area. There is so much confusion about Blue Jacket that it is really hard to know, so I am reserving my decision until I see further evidence.

In any event, Sara Noras Butt, one of the people I discussed before, fits into this family. I believe her to have been Shawnee, and she is related to me through the Greens.

Well, well, well, it looks as though my grandmother who did not want anyone to think she was Indian just might have been.

• Speaking of Sara Noras Butt, another thing you need to watch for is people who are related to you in more than one way. Sarah is my great-great-grandmother Needles, my great-great-aunt Robbins, and a cousin on the Green side.

• Another thing to watch for when reading those family histories is an odd progression. In one of the books on the Needles/Needels family, they go from very early on the Piankatunk River, to Talbot County, Maryland, to Kent and Sussex County, Delaware, to Louisville, Kentucky, and into Indiana before Ohio was settled. Then they return to Ohio. An early west to east progression is unusual and could mean Native people returning after they had moved into another Native area.

You will need to learn to question any type of family activity that does not seem "normal."

My husband's family have a story about an ancestor who found a "German Princess" in Zanesville, Ohio, in the early 1800s. He took her home to his German family and married her. She is buried in the Eppley cemetery under the name Wilhimena. Now, really, a German princess? Just sort of wandering around Zanesville, Ohio? Nah... SO, I went looking for a marriage record. Her name was actually Emanda Riley. I am still trying to get an answer to why the German-speaking Eppleys did not know that Emanda Riley would not be speaking German.

Is it possible that the Eppleys were not German? Another question: they are buried across the road from the German Lutheran Church and cemetery. Why are they not buried in it?

If there is a story told by your people, you can oftentimes look at things they do and begin to see hints of the First American ancestry.

Here are some other things to be aware of, as you search:

• Immigration, especially from England and Germany, is always suspect. Trace those people to the boat, then double check everything to be certain these are truly your people. You must be absolutely certain this person really did come from outside this country. If the person you are researching proves to be European, then check the marriages. Did he or she bring a wife or husband with him or her? If not, did he or she marry in this country? Who, what, where, and when will then apply.

We know that Great-Grandpa was from another country; he was a naturalized citizen. Right? Well, maybe not. Did you know that until 1925, American Indian people were considered foreigners? In their own country. Yes, it is true. Read everything you can concerning the First Americans, and you will come across the law allowing American Indians to be considered American citizens which was passed in 1925. Before 1925, an Indian person living 'outside the reservation had to be naturalized.

• Many First American children were forcefully placed in adoption. There was also the fact that, at removal (that law was passed in 1830), many parents thought it better to leave small children behind than to see them perish on the march, so they gave them to "white" people willing to take them, or they left them with relatives who intended to stay behind. So, adoptions, or the sudden appearance of children too old to belong in the family progression, may show you a First American ancestor.

• The sudden death or disappearance of an ancestor, such as the incident I have given you with Michael Rager. Where did he go and why? People who just seem to fall off the face of the earth may well have had reason to.

• You also want to watch people who just suddenly appear in an area, with no other place where they seem to have been. Why do they have no past?

• Nicknames or middle names that have been handed down through the family which sound sort of "Indian." Things like "White Buck" or just "Buck" for that matter.

• Small towns where everyone is known by a nickname. I once accompanied a friend to her hometown. I believe this town to be a hidden First American town. As we talked to elder people there, they would say, you look familiar, are you from here. She would say, "My father is Floyd Harris."

"I don't think I know him."

"Monk, they called him Monk."

"Oh, sure, I remember Monk, how is he?"

• An ancestor who was considered an outlaw. People who are known not to like strangers; perhaps they kept a shotgun handy to "run off" people they did not know. True outlaws like Jesse James and the Younger Brothers. If you can't earn a decent living in society because of who you are, you might get desperate enough to become an outlaw in order just to live and eat.

• People who were known to be crack shots and extremely good hunters. There is a printed story about a John Rager (I have not found any link between this man and Michael, but Michael's first son is named John) who lived on the Pickaway Plains. He and another man became partners in a hog farm. John was the caretaker. He did not plant any grain and kept half the herd alive through the winter by hunting and feeding them deer. Sound "white" to you?

• Unusual ways of worship. My great-grandmother had all of her grandchildren frightened of her because she "went out into the fields and spoke with the spirits."

• People with an extensive knowledge of herbs and healing. There are people within my knowledge who can stop blood from flowing with a touch, or make a hand go hot or cold by holding it.

• The knowledge and use of herbal medicines.

• Knowledge and use of traditional foods. Drying foodstuffs. Keeping root vegetables such as potatoes and carrots in a "root cellar" or burying them.

• Watch carefully for "verbal clueing." This practice will repeatedly give you a certain story from a relative, when you ask a certain question in just the right way. If you run into such a situation, re-ask the question several times to be certain and then count it as a clue.

Because of verbal clueing, you will find such strange things as the aunt who first told the story of Snow Flower and later asked why she was never told of the Native ancestry.

• Shifting your interest is one of the many ways First American people used to confuse someone who showed too much interest. Claiming that the "Indian" was someone else.

Let me give you an example of that. Not long ago, I went to my hometown to see if I could get some confirmation from the Green family about my theory concerning George and Diadema. I found the oldest living Green descendant in his garage. I told him I was a Green descendant, as well, and I wanted to ask him a few questions about the family. He gave me the name of his great-grandfather, who is my great-great-grandfather, so I know we are talking about the right family. We talked for a little bit and then I asked the big question, "What can you tell me about the Indian ancestry in the Green family?"

His answer, "I know there is dark blood in the Greens, but I don't want to discuss it."

Later, he said, "Well, honey, what you need to do is go to Croton. That family is a totally different clan. They are the Indians."

Now, I have the Green genealogy, so I know they are all the same line, but, just to see what would happen, I traveled to Croton, found a Green descendant there, and got: "Well, honey, you need to go to Johnstown. That family is not related to us, and they are the Indians."

I have a pet theory about these two towns. Johnstown is on a main crossroads. Two state routes cross right in the center of town. Croton is seven miles down a back road from Johnstown. I believe, when removal became a fact, the people who were too dark-skinned to pass for "white" went to live in Croton. Further argument for that is that most people in Croton are related to families in Johnstown.

The history of Croton states that, when it was time to name the town everyone living there was named Crow. So it was called Crow Town and later the w's were dropped. Try to tell me that this is a "white" way to name a town.

• Watch your family stories for "typical frontier women" who smoke pipes. Native people believe that smoke carries your words to creator. Pipe smoking was one way to make certain the Creator knew you were sincere.

• Watch, also, for men or women who belonged to pipe smoking clubs or societies.

• Here are some physical characteristics to watch for:

Type "O" blood can be an indication of First American ancestry. Scientist are beginning to believe that before the advent of the European, "O" may have been the only blood type on this continent.

It is said that First American peoples first came to this continent across the Bering Straits from Siberia. I am certain that some did do that very thing, so "the Mongolian Bruise" becomes a sign of ancestry for some, but not all, First American people. This is a bluish area found on the back of a newborn just above the crack of the buttocks.

There are five major diseases known to be more prevalent in First American People than in the general population. These are: alcoholism — everyone knows about the "Drunken Indian"; arthritis, including fibromyalgia; diabetes; heart disease; and kidney problems, including kidney stones. If two or more of these health problems are present within your family, you probably have First American ancestry. You need to research.

Very often I am told, "But, they don't look Indian." Well, we must remember that the "Indian" we all recognize is Hollywood's version.

Oh, yes, there were headdress-wearing, fringed buckskin-dressed warriors with long jet black braided hair. Dark skinned, very dark brown eyed and solemn. They were the Plains People. There are still many, and they are lucky enough to know who they are. These people lived on the Great Plains, where they received lots and lots of sunlight. It was necessary for them to develop the protection of darker pigmentation.

Back east, however, the Woodland People were called that because they lived in the woods. You don't need very dark skin if you are not exposed to the sun all day every day. If you live under the trees, the need is not as intense. Therefore many "Indian" people did not develop that easily recognizable dark coloring.

There is also the fact that there was contact many years before Columbus. There is very good evidence that Viking contact was made in North America, along the northeast coast. We have always been an accepting race. Differences did not mean as much to our early people as they mean today. Big blond men did intermarry with our women early on. There were red-headed, blue eyed "Indian" people. Also blondes and those with light brown hair. Green and hazel eyes were not unheard of. In *Letters and Notes on the North American Indians*, George Catlin speaks of the blue-eyed Mandans.

There is no reason to believe that because Great-Grandma was a large blond, blue-eyed woman, there is no "Indian" blood there. If your family story says she is the one, then either it is true, or one of her parents was. It does happen that the stories may be off a generation or two.

Once you have established the side of your family known to have First American ancestry, always check the other side. I have seen it happen over and over. Blood attracts blood, even without knowing.

My mother's family are having a hard time accepting my belief that they also have First American ancestry. They claim to be "Pennsylvania Dutch." They have given me many reasons for their belief, primarily in

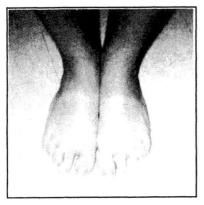

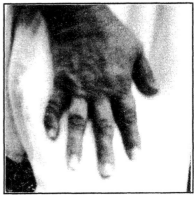

Above: a little toe that lies under the next toe. A second toe that is longer than the big toe. A wider than normal division between the big toe and the second one.
Below: large, heavy earlobes.

Above: crooked fingers.
Below: slightly slanted, almost oriental-appearing eyes. An extra fold in the eyelid, making it appear "heavy" or fat.

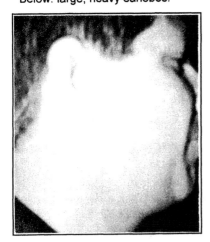

An inverted breastbone, normally called a "chicken breast."

the foods they like and use. Well, First American people did adapt. The "white" man brought many wonders, and we used them.

OK, Pennsylvania Dutch is a euphemism for Amish. There are no Amish beliefs in this family. At no time can I find an Amish person. The family comes from Northumberland County, Pennsylvania. Also Wyoming Valley.

Often, you can look at church affiliations and have a very good idea about what tribe your family belonged to. For instance, the Methodists were missionaries to the Shawnee. I recently saw a Methodist Hymnal with translations into several First American languages.

The Moravians and the United Brethren were Missionaries to the Delaware.

The Lutherans appear to have been missionaries to both the Wyandot and the Shawnee.

After the betrayal of the Removal Act, First American people who stayed behind had every right to be suspicious of outsiders. From 1830 on, they stayed to themselves and married within the group.

These people most often went into the hills and hollers in southern Ohio, northern Kentucky, and West Virginia. They changed their clothes and their lifestyle, and pretended to be "white" or "black" or "mulatto," whatever the color of the skin would allow.

So, you can still find people of almost pure First American ancestry in these areas. I am certain there are other such areas; these are the ones I know about.

OK, now you say, "But, my family is black and they were slaves in the deep South, but they tell this story."

Do not despair. Even though I have had very little experience with black First American ancestry, I do have some words of encouragement.

For those of you whose black ancestry does not go into the deep South and slavery, the hints I have given above will work for you.

For those of you whose ancestry does, here are some little known facts.

The Reader's Digest's book *Through Indian Eyes* states that during the 1700s and early 1800s many Mexican Indian peoples were sold as slaves.

In another part the book gives the number of First American people who were sold through the North and South Carolina slave markets. There were 12,000 Apalachees and Timucuas.

Columbus took First American peoples from the Caribbean Islands back to Spain as slaves in the 1490s and early 1500s.

It is a well known fact that the Seminole people took in escaped slaves and made them part of their tribe, during those times.

People of New England tribes were sold into slavery by the English.

There would always have been intermarriages. One of the things the First American people found most fascinating about the Lewis and Clark expedition was the large black man who was with them. I believe both Alan Eckart and James Alexander Thom refer to him.

So, do not give up. The search may be hard, but hang in there. If you have a family story, it is most likely to be true.

Take the same steps that I have outlined for others. I do realize that your search may be limited if you are old South. But do have the story written down, signed, dated, and notarized. You will still have that going for you, and if you show old South and can go no further, you should still be able to gain acceptance.

As to acceptance, many people (myself included) wish to know their ancestors and to learn as much as possible about the old ways. So, they find the ancestry and run right out and join a Native group. Let me give you some advice about this. I learned this the hard way; I'd like to make things easier for you.

For five years, I was a member of what I thought was a true "tribal" group, only to find that what I was a part of was actually a hobbyist organization. I should like to save you that experience, if I can.

Unfortunately, there are many unscrupulous people in today's Native American world.

There are people who prey on the innocent desire of newly discovered ancestry and claim to be what they are not.

There are people claiming to be "Indian" who have no ancestry, but who have built organizations by convincing others that they are truly Native.

There are true Natives who prey on the desire of the people they term "wannabees" and feed that desire, for money. In actuality, people of true First American intent give freely of their knowledge. They never charge. They will tell you that what is freely given will come back ten-fold.

It is acceptable, but not required, to give someone who is helping you a gift in return for his or her help. There are no particular gifts "required" for any particular service. If you run into a person who does "require" a certain gift for a service, either he or she is not truly Native, or he or she is not giving you correct information. Gifts of tobacco, especially for advice, are always acceptable.

There are "Black Magic" societies and a particularly virulent form of witchcraft rampant in today's Native American world. You must be extremely careful not to get involved with these people.

One of the most important things that I can say to you is to be particularly careful of your children. These groups tend to try to separate the children from the parents. If they hold "camps" in which the children are away from home and parents, if they hold "classes" in which the children are, again, separated from the parents, take the children and leave. You need to be where you can watch what goes on at all times.

Read, read, read. The more you know the less likely you are to innocently become a part of something you do not want to belong to.

There is new information being printed every day. Most of it is very good. I would caution you, however, to carefully check the sources, just to be certain the authors do "know their stuff."

When you do decide to become a part of a Native group, give yourself plenty of time. Watch and check them from every angle. If you have ANY doubts, don't join.

There are certain things that should be done by any group claiming to be a tribe. If you are well read, you will know how these things should be handled. If you see that they are not being handled in that way, don't join.

The most important thing that I can tell you is that First American Councils were always held in the open. There were never any "closed" or "secret" councils. If the group you are looking at holds councils behind closed doors, they are not true First American people. Not even a "closed" council followed by an "open" one is correct. Councils were for the good of all, and were open to all. You could not just go in and speak your piece — you had to be invited to do that — but you were allowed to sit in while your Clan Chief or Clan Mother did the speaking.

Clan Chiefs and Clan Mothers were there to represent their people. They were always chosen by the Clan members. If you are not given a voice, this is not a true "Tribe." Do not join.

If you are looking at joining a Tribe, and they are doing such things as requiring reserved seating at their functions, joining country clubs in the tribal name, demanding money or dues and telling you how much you should be paying, or installing members of council without allowing the clan and tribal body a vote, these things would never have been done in a First American setting. Do not join.

Native American life was always open and free. The people were never told not to speak with this one or that one, etc. Or "Do not read this book, or that book" or "This person or that person does not know what he is talking about." It was ALWAYS left up to the individual involved to make up his or her own mind.

Well, I have given you everything that I have learned so far in working with First American genealogies. I pray that what I have said will be a help to you, and I wish you Happy Hunting.

Following is a listing of names that were taken by First American people and which then appeared in print as Native, along with a listing of areas known to be places where certain types of First American peoples were.

,

NATIVE NAMES

(Primarily Ohio Valley, West Virginia, Virginia, Indiana)

This is a listing of translated names which have been documented as First American. It is by no means complete; nor does it indicate that all people with one of these surnames are First American. For example, many people of English heritage are also named Brown, Williams, or Smith. Researchers are encouraged to consult other records and sources and to pay particular attention to time and place when using this list.

Note: Cty in these listings stands for County

NAME .... TRIBE .... AREA .... DATE

A

Name	Tribe	Area	Date
Aaron	Pequot	Connecticut	
Abbott	Shawnee Rolls		1866
Abby	Koasati		
About	Chippewa Treaty	Mackinack Island	1815
Abraham	Choctaw	Hopewell, TN	1785
	Seminole		1894
Ackerman	Delaware	Oklahoma	
Acorn	Cherokee Treaty	Banks of Holston, TN	1791
Actor	Wyandot Treaty	Spring Wells	1815
Adair	Cherokee Census		1835
Adams	Melungeon	NC, VA, TN, KY	
	Pamunkey/Powhatan	Virginia	
	Guineas	West Virginia	
	Wyandot Treaty	Greenville, OH	1795
Adkins	Melungeon	NC, VA, TN, KY	
	Pamunkey/Powhatan	Virginia	

NAME	TRIBE	AREA	DATE
Adolpha	Flathead		
Ahenakew	Plains Cree		
Aikens	Comanche		
Ajo	Mohawk Treaty	New York	1797
Albough	Delaware	Oklahoma	
Alder	Shawnee	Greenville, OH	1817
Aleck	Creek Treaty	New York City	1790
Alexander	Kalispel		
Alewai	Tsimshian		
Alford	Absentee Shawnee Rolls		1934
Allen	Lumbee/Croatan	North & South Carolina	
Allmond	Pamunkey/Powhatan	Virginia	
Almighty	Chippewa Treaty	Spring Wells	1815
Amason	Aluet		
American	Wyandot Treaty	Lake Erie	1817
Anderson	Shawnee	Meigs Cty, OH	1795
	Melungeon		
	Delaware	Greenville, OH	1795
	Miami Treaty	St. Marys, OH	1818
	Wyandot Treaty	Greenville, OH	
Andrews	Delaware	Kansas	1858
Anguhadlug	Inuit		
	Tailrunili		
Annesley	Cherokee		
Antonio	Cahuilla		
Antonis	Delaware	Anadarko, OK	1876
Apaumat	Listed "Christian Indian"	New York	1790s
Apes	Pequot	Connecticut	
Apaumet	Mohican		
Apperance	Osage Treaty	Spring Wells	1815
Arab	Melungeon		

NAME ....*TRIBE*............*AREA* ....*DATE*

Arch	Cherokee Census		1835
Archer	Shawnee	Meigs Cty, OH	1887
	Powhatan	Virginia	
Archseit	Cherokee Census		1835
Arm	Wyandot Treaty	Greenville, OH	1814
(Tattooed Arm)	Natchez		
Arms	Seneca	Sandusky Cty, OH	1817
Armstrong	Wyandot	Land Grant	1817
	Delaware	Darke Cty, OH	1795
	Ottawa Treaty	St. Marys, OH	1818
Arna	Seminole	Florida	1893
Arnold	Delaware	Oklahoma	
Arrow(s)	Six Nations Treaty	Ft. Harmar, OH	1789
	Creek Treaty	New York City	1790
	Cherokee Treaty	Tellico, TN	1805
	Wyandot Treaty	Ft. McIntosh	1785
	Blackfeet		
	Seneca		
Ash	Seneca	Sandusky Cty, OH	1817
	Shawnee Rolls		1895
Ashawet	Ottawa	Lake Erie	1814
Ashby	Potawatomi		
Ashworth	Redbones	Louisiana	
Asisara	Santa Cruz		
Attucks	Massachuset		1776
Augustin	Pomo		
Aumiller	Shawnee	Meigs Cty, OH	1859
Ayers	Catawba		
Axe	Oneida Treaty	New York	1794
Azul	Pima		

NAME .... *TRIBE* .... *AREA* .... *DATE*

B

Name	Tribe	Area	Date
Babcock	Pequot	Connecticut	
Bad (Bad Heart Bull)	Ottawa Treaty Lakota	Greenville, OH	1795
Badger	Cherokee Treaty	Banks of Holston, TN	1791
Badgerson	Cherokee Treaty	Tellico, TN	1805
Bake	Navajo		
Baker	Shawnee Mohegan Hidasta	Darke Cty, OH	1817
Bald	Cherokee Treaty Ottawa Treaty	Tellico, TN St. Marys, OH	1805 1818
Bale	Six Nations Treaty	Ft. Harmar, OH	1789
Ball	Ottawa Treaty	Detroit, MI	1807
Bandie	Miami Treaty	Greenville, OH	1814
Banks	Ojibwa		
Baptista (Baptiste)	Shawnee	Darke Cty, OH	1814
Bare	Shawnee	Mason Cty, KY	1820
Bark	Cherokee Treaty	Tellico, TN	1805
Barker	Shawnee Melungeon Delaware	Mason Cty, WV NC, VA, TN, KY	1862
Barlowe	Powhatan	Virginia	
Barnard	Creek Treaty	Ft. Wilkinson	1802
Barnes	Melungeon	NC, VA, TN, KY	
Barnett	Wyandot Treaty	Spring Wells	1815
Baron	Shawnee Treaty	Limestone, KY	1820
Barren	Shawnee Treaty	Limestone, KY	1820
Bascomb	Delaware	Kansas	1867
Basket	Seneca	Sandusky Cty, OH	1817

NAME	TRIBE	AREA	DATE
Bass	Shawnee	Meigs Cty, OH	1829
		Mason Cty, WV	1829
	Pamunkey/Powhatan	Virginia	
Bastard	Ottawa Treaty	Spring Wells	1815
Bat	Cheyenne		
Baty	Shawnee	Meigs Cty, OH	1829
(Beatey/Beaty)		Mason Cty, WV	1829
Baube	Wyandot Treaty	Greenville, OH	1814
Bean	Melungeon	Hawkins Cty, TN	
	Cherokee		
Bear	Cherokee Treaty	Banks of Holston, TN	1791
(Bear's Paw)	Delaware	Missouri	1818
	Ottawa Treaty	Vincennes, IN	1805
	Chippewa Treaty	Brownsville, NY	1808
	Potawatomi Treaty		1814
	Miami Treaty	St. Marys, OH	1818
(Standing Bear)	Lakota		
(Bear's Arm)	Hidasta		
(Fire Bear)	Assiniboin		1900
(Bear Ghost)	Blackfoot		1826
	Ponca		
	Sauk		
Bearcup	Sioux		
Beard	Oneida Treaty	New York	1794
	Shawnee		
Bearrer	Cherokee		
Bearskin	Wyandot	Crawford Cty, OH	1832
Beaubien	Miami	Darke Cty, OH	1814
Beaver	Miami	Darke Cty, OH	1795
	Delaware	Greenville, OH	1795
		Muskingum Valley, OH	1758
	Osage Treaty	Spring Wells	1815
	Winnebago		
Beckler	Melungeon	NC, VA, TN, KY	

NAME ....*TRIBE*........................*AREA* ....*DATE*

Name	Tribe	Area	Date
Beckworth	Crow		
	Blackfoot		
Bedoka	Caddo-Delaware		
Beecroft	Delaware		
Begay	Navajo		
Begood	Redbones	LA via the Carolinas	
Beiner	Delaware	Oklahoma	
Belknap	Delaware	Oklahoma	
Bell	Melungeon	NC, VA, TN, KY	
	Shawnee Rolls		1895
	Wyandot Treaty	Greenville, OH	1814
	Seminole	Florida	
Bellecourt	Ojibwa		
Belly	Miami	Darke Cty, OH	1814
	Potawatomi Treaty		1814
Belt	Seneca	Sandusky Cty, OH	1817
Ben	Miami Treaty	St. Marys, OH	1818
Bender	Delaware	Oklahoma	
Benjamin	Wyandot Treaty	Forks of Wabash, IN	1842
Bennett	Lumbee/Croatan	North & South Carolina	
	Melungeon	NC, VA, TN, KY	
	Oneida		
Bent	Arapaho		
Benenhaley	Melungeon		
Bergschicken	Shawnee	Meigs Cty, OH	1836
Berndt	Delaware	Oklahoma	
Berry	Seneca	Sandusky Cty, OH	1817
	Lumbee/Croatan	North & South Carolina	
	Melungeon	NC, VA, TN, KY	
	Keetoowah (Cherokee)		
	Shawnee		
Betancourt	Seneca		

NAME	TRIBE	AREA	DATE
Betsy	Delaware Omaha	Anadarko, OK	1876
Between (Between the Logs)	Wyandot Treaty Osage Treaty	Greenville, OH Spring Wells	1814 1815
Beverly	Pamunkey/Powhatan	Virginia	
Bevers	Shawnee		1817
Big	Creek Treaty	New York City	1790
	Cherokee Treaty	Banks of Holston, TN	1791
	Shawnee Treaty	Wapakoneta, OH	1831
	Oneida Treaty	New York	1794
	Eel River Treaty	Vincennes, IN	1803
(Bigtree)	Ottawa Treaty	Vincennes, IN	1805
	Ottawa Treaty	Detroit, MI	1807
	Chippewa Treaty	Greenville, OH	1815
	Miami Treaty	St. Marys, OH	1818
(Big Ankle)	Sioux		
(Big Mouth)	Onondaga		
(Big Foot)	Sioux		
	Seminole	Florida	1875
Bigby	Cherokee Census		1836
Biggs	Melungeon	NC, VA, TN, KY	
Biggers	Melungeon		
Bighead	Cheyenne		
Bill	Delaware	Kansas	1864
	Seneca Treaty	Lewistown, OH	1831
Billie	Seminole Miccosukee	Florida	
Billy	Oneida Treaty	New York	1794
	Wyandot Treaty	Greenville, OH	1795
	Seneca Treaty	Buffalo Creek, NY	1802
	Pomo		
	Seminole	Florida	1862
Birch	Shawnee	Meigs Cty, OH	1894
Bird(s)	Shawnee	Pike Cty, OH	1815
	Cherokee Treaty	Banks of Holston, TN	1791
	Ottawa Treaty	Greenville, OH	1791

NAME .... *TRIBE* .... *AREA* .... *DATE*

Name	Tribe	Area	Date
Bird(s) *(continued)*			
	Osage Treaty	Spring Wells	1815
	Creek		
	Blackfeet		
	Crow		
	Sioux		
	Nez Perce		
	Sauk		
	Winnebago		
Birdtail	Creek Treaty	New York City	1790
Bisangee	Seminole	Florida	1886
Black	Creek Treaty		1814
(Blacktom)	Delaware	Muskingum Valley, OH	1772
	Kickapoo Treaty	Greenville, OH	1814
	Osage Treaty	Spring Wells	1815
	Cherokee Treaty	Banks of Holston, TN	1791
	Ottawa Treaty	St. Marys, OH	1818
	Shawnee Treaty	Greenville, OH	1795
	Eel River Treaty	Vincennes, IN	1803
(Black Elk)	Oglala		
(Black Hawk)	Sauk		
(Black Moon)	Hunkpapa		
(Black Thunder)	Fox		
(Black Kettle)	N. Cheyenne		
	Potawatomi		
Blackbeard	Wyandot		
Blackbird	Ottawa	Chicago, IL	1790
Blacketer	Shawnee Rolls		1896
Blain	Shawnee	Meigs Cty, OH	
Blair	Cherokee/Shawnee	Morgan Cty, KY	1860
	Delaware	Oklahoma	
Blake	Hidasta		
Blanc	Ottawa Treaty	Detroit, MI	1807
Blank	Shawnee	Meigs Cty, OH	1886
Blankenship	Delaware	Oklahoma	

NAME .... *TRIBE* .... *AREA* .... *DATE*

Blanket	Delaware	Anadarko, OK	1876
	Kickapoo Treaty		1814
	Wyandot Treaty	St. Marys, OH	1818
	Cherokee		
	Sauk		
Blast	Six Nations Treaty	Ft. Harmar, OH	1789
Blind	Seminole	Florida	1835
Blood	Blackfeet		
Bloody	Cherokee Treaty	Banks of Holston, TN	1791
Blow (Blow Snake)	Winnebago		
Blower	Osage Treaty		1815
Blue	Creek Treaty	New York City	1790
	Seneca Treaty	Buffalo Creek, NY	1802
	Shawnee Treaty	Greenville, OH	1805
Blunt	Seminole		
Board	Seneca		
Bobb (Bob)	Delaware	Kansas	1864
Body	Seneca	Sandusky Cty, OH	1817
	Blackfeet		
Boggs	Shawnee	Mason Cty, WV	1893
	Cherokee Census		1835
Bold	Cherokee Treaty	Banks of Holston, TN	1791
Bolen	Melungeon	NC, VA, TN, KY	
Bolesle	Wyandot Treaty	Greenville, OH	1814
Boling	Powhatan	Virginia	
Bolling	Wyandot		
Bonamico	Delaware	Oklahoma	
Bonaventure	Coeur d' Alene		
Bone	Wyandot Treaty	St. Marys, OH	1818
Boney	Pequot	Connecticut	
Bonnin	Sioux		

NAME .... *TRIBE*..................... *AREA* .... *DATE*

Name	Tribe	Area	Date
Boone	Brass Ankles	North Carolina	
Boots	Cherokee Treaty	Banks of Holston, TN	1791
Borling	Melungeon		
Boruta	Delaware	Oklahoma	
Bosomworth	Creek		1752
Boudinot	Cherokee		
Bourassa	Choctaw		
Bowers	Wyandot Treaty	Greenville, OH	1814
Bowl (Big)	Ottawa Cherokee	Vincennes, IN	1805
Bowlegs	Seminole	Florida	1862
Bowlin	Melungeon		
Bowling	Melungeon	Hawkins Cty, TN	
Bowman	Melungeon Shawnee	NC, VA, TN, KY Flatrock, IN	1820
Box	Sioux		
Boy	Cherokee Treaty Wyandot Treaty Ottawa Treaty Blackfeet	Tellico, TN Vincennes, IN Vincennes, IN	1805 1805 1805
Boyer	Shawnee Delaware Wyandot Treaty	Muskingum Valley, OH St. Marys, OH	1773 1818
Bozarth	Shawnee		
Bradby	Pamunkey/Powhatan	Virginia	
Brand	Mohawk Seneca Treaty	Muskingum Valley, OH Greenville, OH	1789 1814
Branham	Melungeon	NC, VA, TN, KY	
Brant	Mohawk	Muskingum Valley, OH	1789
Brashears	Choctaw		
Braveboy	Brass Ankles	South Carolina	
Bread	Blackfeet		

NAME ....*TRIBE*........................*AREA* ....*DATE*

Breast	Blackfeet		
Breath	Osage Treaty	Spring Wells	1816
Brend	Pequot	Connecticut	
Brice	Shawnee		
Brickle	Delaware		
Bridger	Lumbee/Croatan	North & South Carolina	
Briger	Lumbee/Croatan	North & South Carolina	
Briggs	Delaware	Oklahoma	
Bright	Shawnee	Meigs Cty, OH	
Brigman	Melungeon		
Brinker	Shawnee	Meigs Cty, OH	1879
Brinton	Powhatan	Virginia	
Brogen	Melungeon	NC, VA, TN, KY	
Broken Knife	Delaware	Kansas	1864
Broken	Six Nations Treaty	New York	1889
	Creek Treaty	New York City	1890
	Oneida Treaty	New York	1794
Broker	Ojibwa		
Brooks	Lumbee/Croatan	North & South Carolina	
Broom	Cherokee Treaty	Tellico, TN	1790
Broth	Cherokee		
	Sauk		
Brother	Oneida Treaty	New York	1784
	Creek Treaty	New York City	1790
	Seneca Treaty	Genesee River, NY	1802
	Wyandot Treaty	Spring Wells	1815
Brothertown	Pequot	Connecticut	
Brown	Wyandot	Ft. Sandusky, OH	1805
	Delaware	Kansas	1864
	Lumbee/Croatan	North & South Carolina	
	Shawnee Rolls		1896
	Choctaw Treaty	Chickasaw Bluffs	1801
	Cherokee Census		1835

NAME .... *TRIBE* .... *AREA* .... *DATE*

Name	Tribe	Area	Date
Brunn	Delaware	Oklahoma	
Buck	Seneca	Sandusky Cty, OH	1817
	Delaware	Missouri	1818
	Miami Treaty	St. Marys, OH	1818
	Shawnee Treaty	Wapakoneta, OH	1831
	Seminole	Florida	1850
Buckholts	Choctaw		
Buckhorn	Seminole	Florida	1858
Buckler	Powhatan	Virginia	
Buckman	Potawatomi		
Buckwheat	Delaware	Darke Cty, OH	1785
Buehler	Delaware	Oklahoma	
Buffalo	Delaware	Darke Cty, OH	1795
	Choctaw Treaty	Hopewell, TN	1786
	Wyandot Treaty	Greenville, OH	1795
	Creek Treaty		
(Buffalo Bird Woman)	Hidasta		
(Buffalo Calf Woman)	Cheyenne		
(Sitting Buffalo)	Hunkpapa		
(White Buffalo)	Fox		
	Blackfeet		
Buffington	Cherokee Census		1835
Bufort	Osage Treaty	Spring Wells	1815
Bug	Six Nations Treaty	Ft. Harmar, OH	1789
Bull	Delaware	Anadarko, OK	1876
(Bad Heart Bull)	Sioux		
	Blackfeet		
	N. Cheyenne		
	Piankeshaw		
Bullet(s)	Delaware	Muskingum Valley, OH	1764
	Wea Treaty	Grouseland, IN	1805
Bullion	Melungeon	NC, VA, TN, KY	
Bunch	Melungeon		
	Shawnee		
	Brass Ankles	South Carolina	

NAME .... *TRIBE* .... *AREA* .... *DATE*

NAME	TRIBE	AREA	DATE
Bunning	Delaware	Oklahoma	
Burch	Delaware	Oklahoma	
Burner	Shawnee Potawatomi		
Burnett	Potawatomi	Michigan	1798
Burris	Powhatan	Virginia	
Burton	Melungeon Cherokee	NC, VA, TN, KY	1910
Bush	Absentee Shawnee Delaware	Oklahoma	
Bushyhead	Cherokee Census		1835
Buskenuggee	Seminole	Florida	1860
Buster	Seminole	Florida	1875
Butler	Lumbee/Croatan Cherokee Shawnee	North & South Carolina Kentucky Auglaize Cty, OH	1819
Butter	Wyandot Treaty	Greenville, OH	1814
Butterfly	Osage Treaty Cherokee Treaty Wyandot Treaty	Spring Wells Tellico, TN Spring Wells	1815 1798 1815
Butters	Redbones	Louisiana	
Buxton	Redbones	Louisiana	
Byrd	Melungeon Powhatan	NC, VA, TN, KY Virginia	
Bysaw	Seneca	Sandusky Cty, OH	1817

ℂ

NAME	TRIBE	AREA	DATE
Cabin	Cherokee Treaty Choctaw Treaty	Banks of Holston, TN Hopewell, TN	1791 1786
Cadotte	Chippewa		
Caghkoo	Delaware	Missouri	1818

NAME .... *TRIBE* .... *AREA* .... *DATE*

Name	Tribe	Area	Date
Caldwell	Seminole Ottawa Ogee		
Calf	Choctaw Treaty Blackfeet	Hopewell, TN	1786
Calloe	Melungeon		
Canady	Seneca Shawnee	New York Mason Cty, WV	1793
Camba	Miami	Darke Cty, OH	1814
Campbell	Melungeon	NC, VA, TN, KY	
Canasateego	Onondaga		
Candy	Cherokee Census		1835
Canoe(s) (Dragging Canoe)	Six Nations Treaty Cherokee Mohawk	Hopewell, TN	1786
Capes	Shawnee	Allen Cty, OH	1817
Capps	Delaware	Kansas	1864
Captain	Wyandot Treaty Oneida Treaty Wea Treaty Delaware Treaty Shawnee Treaty Miami Treaty Piankashaw	Greenville, OH New York Grouseland, IN Ft. Wayne, IN Greenville, OH St. Marys, OH	1795 1794 1805 1809 1814 1818
Capture	Arapaho Gros Ventre	Montana	
Carey	Seminole	Florida	1899
Carlson	Delaware	Oklahoma	
Carlton	Shawnee	Meigs Cty, OH	
Carlyle	Delaware	Kansas	1858
Carmack	Tagish		
Carnes	Choctaw Treaty	Mt. Dexter	1805
Carney	Delaware	Roane Cty, WV	

NAME .... *TRIBE* .... *AREA* .... *DATE*

Name	Tribe	Area	Date
Carp	Ottawa		
Carpenter	Seneca Treaty	Lewistown, OH	1831
	Shawnee Rolls		1832
	Pequot	Connecticut	
	Cherokee		
Carrico	Melungeon	NC, VA, TN, KY	
Carrier	Oneida Treaty	New York	1794
	Six Nations Treaty	Philadelphia, PA	1794
Carson	Shawnee	Meigs Cty, OH	1844
Carter	Pamunkey/Powhatan	Virginia	
	Melungeon	NC, VA, TN, KY	
Cassacinamon	Pequot	Connecticut	
Cassadore	Apache		
Cassman	Delaware	Missouri	1818
Casteel	Melungeon	NC, VA, TN, KY	
Cat	Delaware	Missouri	1818
(Catfish)	Ottawa Treaty	Vincennes, IN	1805
	Kickapoo Treaty	Ft. Wayne, IN	1803
Catcher	Cherokee Treaty	Banks of Holston, TN	1791
Caton	Shawnee	Meigs Cty, OH	
Caudill	Melungeon	NC, VA, TN, KY	
Cavallo	Seminole	Florida	
Cayoete	N. Cheyenne		
Cedar	Ottawa Treaty	Detroit, MI	1807
	Wyandot Treaty	Lake Erie	1817
Centeno	Chumash		
Chambers	Cherokee Census		1832
Chapman	Lumbee/Croatan	North & South Carolina	
	Delaware	Oklahoma	
Charles	Pequot	Connecticut	
Charley	Miami	Darke Cty, OH	1814
	Eel River Treaty	Vincennes, IN	1803
	Cherokee		

NAME ....TRIBE.......................AREA ....DATE

Charley *(continued)*			
	Seminole	Florida	1892
Charlie	Kickapoo		
	Whitewater		
	Seminole	Florida	1875
Charlo	Ottawa	St. Marys, OH	1831
Chased	Santee		
(Chased by Bears)			
Chatee	Mohawk Treaty	New York	1795
Chavis	Melungeon		
	Redbones	Louisiana	
	Brass Ankles	South Carolina	
	Lumbee/Croatan	North & South Carolina	
Cheek	Cherokee		
	Sauk		
Cherokee	Wyandot Treaty	Vincennes, IN	1805
Chickasaw	Cherokee Treaty	Banks of Holston, TN	1791
Chief	Blackfeet		
	Delaware		
	Cherokee		
	Sauk		
	Seneca	Sandusky Cty, OH	1817
	Wyandot Treaty	Browntown, MI	1808
(Chief Eagle)	Lakota		
	Shawnee	Auglaize Cty, OH	1817
(Chief Eagle)	Teton		
	N. Cheyenne		
Child	Blackfeet		
	Seminole	Florida	1862
Childers	Creek		
(Childres)	Cherokee Census		1835
Chino	Acoma Pueblo		
	Apache		
Chinqua	Delaware	Anadarko, OK	
Chipco	Seminole	Florida	1890

NAME	TRIBE	AREA	DATE
Chipio	Seminole	Florida	1890
Chiricahua	Apache		
Chisolm	Cherokee		
Chopes	Creek Treaty	Georgia	1796
Chouteau	Shawnee Creek		
Chovis	Melungeon		
Chris	Mescalero		1880
Christy	Cherokee Census		1835
Chroasten (Croaston/Crostin)	Melungeon		
Christ	Shawnee	Mason Cty, WV	1820
Churches	Pequot	Connecticut	
Circle (Was originally Zerkle)	Shawnee	Meigs Cty, OH	1874
Circular	Creek Treaty		1814
Civil	Shawnee Treaty Osage Treaty Seneca Treaty	Vincennes, IN Spring Wells Greenville, OH	1805 1815 1814
Clady	Pequot	Connecticut	
Clapper	Melungeon		
Clark	Melungeon Redbones	Louisiana	
Clarke	Wyandot Blackfeet	Crawford Cty, OH	1832
Claw	Cherokee	Clay Cty, KY	
Clay	Shawnee Treaty	Wapakoneta, OH	1831
Clear	Blackfeet		
Clemons	Delaware	Oklahoma	
Clock	Chippewa Treaty	Greenville, OH	1815
Closnee (Closenie)	Cherokee Treaty	Tellico, TN	1805

NAME .... *TRIBE* .... *AREA* .... *DATE*

Cloud(s)	Redbones	Louisiana	
	Wyandot Treaty	Vincennes, IN	1805
	Ottawa Treaty	Detroit, MI	1807
	Chippewa Treaty	Greenville, OH	1815
	Shawnee	Darke Cty, OH	1817
	Blackfeet		
	Sioux		
	Cherokee		
	Sauk		
Coal	Melungeon	NC, VA, TN, KY	
	Shawnee		
	Potawatomi		
Cochise	Chiricahua		1874
Coe	Melungeon		
Coffee	Seneca Treaty	Greenville, OH	1814
	Cherokee Census		1835
	Seminole	Florida	1896
Coffeehouse	Seneca	Sandusky Cty, OH	1817
Coffey	Melungeon	NC, VA, TN, KY	
Cogwood	Cherokee Census		1835
Coheurst	Cherokee Census		1835
Cohena	Cherokee Census		1835
Cohoe	Cheyenne		
Colbert	Shawnee	Trigg Cty, KY	1820
	Choctaw Treaty	Chickasaw Bluffs	1801
	Delaware Treaty	Grouseland, IN	1805
	Chickasaw		1826
	Cherokee		
Cold (Coldwater)	Seneca Treaty	Lewistown, OH	1831
Cole	Melungeon	Hawkins Cty, TN	
	Lumbee/Croatan	North & South Carolina	
Coleman	Melungeon	North & South Carolina	
	Lumbee/Croatan	North & South Carolina	
	Cubans	North Carolina	

NAME ....*TRIBE*............................*AREA* ....*DATE*

Name	Tribe	Area	Date
Colens	Melungeon		
Coles	Melungeon	NC, VA, TN, KY	
Colings	Melungeon		
Colins	Melungeon		
Collector	Osage Treaty	Spring Wells	1815
Colley	Melungeon	NC, VA, TN, KY	
Collier	Melungeon	NC, VA, TN, KY	
	Powhatan	Virginia	
Collins	Shawnee	Meigs Cty, OH	
	Melungeon	Highland Cty, OH	
		Hawkins Cty, TN	
	Delaware	Kansas	1864
	Pamunkey/Powhatan	Virginia	
	Guineas	West Virginia	
Collinsworth	Melungeon	NC, VA, TN, KY	
Colofadas	Mimbreno Apache		
Colonel	Shawnee Treaty	Brownstown, MI	1808
	Ottawa Treaty	St. Marys, OH	1818
Colyer	Melungeon	NC, VA, TN, KY	
Col'mata	Shawnee Rolls		1896
Come	Wyandot Treaty	Greenville, OH	1814
Companies	Seneca	Sandusky Cty, OH	1817
Combs	Shawnee	Monroe Cty, OH	1820
Common	Cherokee Treaty	Banks of Holston, TN	1791
Compston	Delaware	Kansas	1867
Conacene	Cherokee Census		1835
Conepatchie	Seminole	Florida	1860
Conge	Wyandot Treaty	Lake Erie	1817
Conklin	Ponca		
	Osage		
Conn	Potawatomi		
Conneatin	Seneca Treaty	Genesee River, NY	1802

NAME	TRIBE	AREA	DATE
Conner	Shawnee Delaware Cherokee Census	Muskingum Cty, OH	1773 1835
Connie	Seminole	Florida	1893
Consols	Shawnee	Mason Cty, WV	1880
Contrary	Sioux		
Convers	Shawnee	Muskingum Valley, OH	1791
Cooday	Tinglit		
Cook(s)	Delaware Pamunkey/Powhatan Cherokee Census Pequot	Muskingum Valley, OH Virginia Connecticut	1790 1835
Cookson	Cherokee Census		1835
Coon	Wyandot		
Cooper	Lumbee/Croatan	North & South Carolina	
Cooter	Seminole	Florida	1888
Copeland	Delaware	Kansas	1858
Copper	Delaware		
Copway	Ojibwa		
Corder	Wyandot		
Corn (Corntassel)	Shawnee Eel River Treaty Wyandot Treaty Choctaw Treaty Cherokee	Meigs Cty, OH Vincennes, IN Lake Erie Hopewell	 1803 1817 1790
Cornel	Creek Treaty	New York City	1790
Cornells	Creek Treaty	Ft. Wilkinson	1802
Cornelius	Oneida		
Cornplanter	Six Nations Treaty Oneida Treaty Seneca Treaty	Ft. Harmar, OH New York Genesee River, NY	1789 1794 1892
Cornsilk	Cherokee Census		1835
Cornstalk	Shawnee	Allen Cty, OH	1817

NAME .... *TRIBE* .... *AREA* .... *DATE*

Name	Tribe	Area	Date
Cotman	Melungeon	NC, VA, TN, KY	
Cottrell	Pequot	Connecticut	
Coulson	Cherokee Census		1835
Council (Councilkeeper)	Six Nations Treaty	Ft. Harmar, OH	1789
Counts	Melungeon	NC, VA, TN, KY	
Cox(e)	Melungeon	NC, VA, TN, KY	
Coy	Tulalip		
Cozad	Shawnee		
Crayfish	Seneca	Sandusky Cty, OH	1817
Crane	Seneca	Sandusky Cty, OH	1817
	Wyandot	Fairfield Cty, OH	1796
	Cherokee Treaty	Banks of Holston, TN	1791
	Potawatomi Treaty		1814
	Blackfeet		
Crazy Horse	Apache		
Creek	Creek		
Creel	Melungeon		
Creeping	Cherokee Treaty	Tellico, TN	1805
Cresent	Miami	Greenville, OH	1814
Criel	Brass Ankles	South Carolina	
Crispin	Melungeon	Highland Cty, OH	
Crittenden	Cherokee Census		1835
Criss	Shawnee	Mason Cty, WV	1820
Cronin	Delaware	Oklahoma	
Crooked	Creek Treaty		1814
Crosby	Delaware	Oklahoma	
Cross	Six Nations Treaty	Ft. Harmar, OH	1789
	Shawnee Treaty	Greenville, OH	1814
Crosten (Croston)	Melungeon		

NAME	TRIBE	AREA	DATE
Crow	Delaware	Darke Cty, OH	1795
		Muskingum Cty, OH	1795
	Melungeon	NC, VA, TN, KY	
	Wyandot Treaty	Ft. Harmar, OH	1789
	Potawatomi Treaty		1814
	Chippewa Treaty	Grand River, IN	1815
(Crowfoot)	Blackfoot		
	Crow		
	Arikara		
Crumb	Shawnee		
Crutchfield	Cherokee Census		1835
Cub	Wyandot Treaty	Spring Wells	1815
Cullake	Cherokee Census		1835
Cumba	Melungeon	NC, VA, TN, KY	
	Lumbee/Croatan	North & South Carolina	
Cumbow	Lumbee/Croatan	North & South Carolina	
	Melungeon	NC, VA, TN, KY	
Cummings	Delaware	Kansas	1858
Cummins	Delaware	Kansas	1864
Cunningham	Shawnee	Mason Cty, WV	
Cuppahe	Shawnee	Auglaize Cty, OH	1819
Curfee	Wampanoag		
Curleyhead	Delaware	Kansas	1867
Curo	Hopi		
Curry	Melungeon	NC, VA, TN, KY	
Curtis	Shawnee	Meigs Cty, OH	1899
	Delaware	Oklahoma	
	Kansas		
	Osage		
Cusick	Wyandot Treaty	Greenville, OH	1795
Custalow	Pamunkey/Powhatan	Virginia	
Cutter	Blackfeet		
Cypress	Seminole	Florida	1875

NAME .... *TRIBE* .... *AREA* .... *DATE*

D

Name	Tribe	Area	Date
Dagnet	Shawnee Rolls		1867
Daniel	Pequot	Connecticut	
Dalton	Melungeon Guineas	West Virginia	
Dann	Hopi		
Danny	Shawnee	Auglaize Cty, OH	1817
Dam	Shawnee	Darke Cty, OH	1817
Dancing	Six Nations Treaty	Ft. Harmar, OH	1789
Daniel(s)	Cherokee Census Delaware	Oklahoma	1835
Darby	Wyandot	Madison Cty, OH	1774
Dare	Lumbee/Croatan	North & South Carolina	
Daugherty	Cherokee Census Shawnee Rolls		1835 1854
Daughter	Seminole	Florida	1893
David	Mohawk Creek Treaty Hopi Shawnee	Muskingum, OH New York City Auglaize Cty, OH	1778 1790 1817
Davidson	Haida Wyandot		
Davis	Shawnee Melungeon Cherokee Treaty Delaware	Meigs Cty, OH NC, VA, TN, KY Tellico, TN	1856 1805
Dawson	Wyandot Tagish Delaware	Sandusky Cty, OH	1842
Day	Shawnee Delaware	Tippeconoe Cty, IN Oklahoma	1820
Deal	Navajo		

NAME .... *TRIBE* .... *AREA* .... *DATE*

Name	Tribe	Area	Date
Dean	Delaware		
Deavers	Wyandot		
De Chicora	Calusa		
De Cora	Winnebago		
Deer	Menominee Sauk		
Defreese	Melungeon		
Defries	Delaware	Kansas	
De La Clara	Pueblo		
De Lahontan	Powhatan	Virginia	
Deloria	Sioux		
De Groat	Melungeon		
Delp	Melungeon		
Denham	Melungeon		
Dennis	Pamunkey/Powhatan Colville Seminole	Virginia Florida	 1881
Dennison	Delaware	Oklahoma	
Deshane	Shawnee Rolls		1854
Desjarlais	Chippewa		
DeSoto	Seminole	Florida	1881
Dessecker	Delaware	Oklahoma	
Devil	Wyandot Treaty Seminole	Spring Wells Florida	1815 1840
Diablo	White Mountain Apache Mohawk		
Dial	Lumbee/Croatan	North & South Carolina	
Dick	Delaware Melungeon Cherokee Treaty Pequot	Missouri Highland Cty, OH Tellico, TN Connecticut	1818 1805
Diebold	Seneca Cayuga		

NAME .... *TRIBE* .... *AREA* .... *DATE*

Diebold *(continued)*	Shawnee		
Difficulty	Miami	Greenville, OH	1814
Dillow	Wyandot		
Di Sable	Potawatomi	Illinois	
Disputer	Cowetas Treaty	New York	1790
Disturber	Cherokee Treaty	Banks of Holston, TN	1791
Dixie	Seminole	Florida	1878
Doctor	Wyandot Treaty	Sandusky	1842
(Curly Headed Doctor)	Modoc		
	Seminole	Florida	1850
Dodge	Navajo		
Dog(s)	Ottawa	Lake Erie	1805
	Eel River Treaty	Vincennes, IN	1803
	Wyandot Treaty	Spring Wells	1815
	Oneida Treaty	New York	1794
	Six Nations Treaty	Ft. Harmar, OH	1789
(Fire Dog)	Cheyenne		
	Blackfeet		
Dondee	Delaware	Greenville, OH	1814
Dorman	Sioux		
Dorton	Melungeon		
	Guineas	West Virginia	
Double			
(Doublehead)	Cherokee Treaty	Banks of Holston, TN	1781
(Doubletooth)	Creek Treaty	Tellico, TN	1814
Douds	Delaware	Oklahoma	
Doughtery	Cherokee Treaty	Tellico, TN	1805
	Winnebago		
Doughty	Delaware	Muskingum Cty, OH	1812
Douglas	Cree		
	Wampanoag		
Dow	Shawnee	Meigs Cty, OH	1866
Dowdy	Cherokee/Shawnee	Grayson Cty, KY	1892

NAME .... *TRIBE* .... *AREA* .... *DATE*

Name	Tribe	Area	Date
Down	Seneca	Sandusky	1817
	Wyandot Treaty	Greenville, OH	1814
Downey	Pueblo		
Downing	Cherokee Census		1835
Doyle	Redbones	Louisiana	
Drag or Dragging (Dragging Canoe)	Cherokee		
Dragoo	Ottawa	Muskingum Valley, OH Licking Cty, OH	1808
Dreadfull	Cherokee Treaty	Tellico, TN	1805
Dreamer	Modoc		
Drennen	Shawnee		
Driggers	Brass Ankles	South Carolina	
Drinkwater	Melungeon		
Driver	Wyandot	Crawford Cty, OH	1832
Drumm	Delaware	Oklahoma	
Dry	Creek Treaty	New York City	1790
Duchouguet	Shawnee	Auglaize Cty, OH	1817
Duck (Wildduck)	Kickapoo Treaty Seneca	Sandusky Cty, OH	1814 1817
Ducoigne	Eel River Treaty	Vincennes, IN	1803
Duncan	Delaware Shawnee Rolls Cherokee Census	Muskingum Valley, OH	1773 1877 1835
Duley	Comanche		
Dunham	Delaware	Oklahoma	
Dunlavy	Shawnee	Meigs Cty, OH	1894
Dutch	Cherokee		
Dye	Melungeon	NC, VA, TN, KY	
Dyess	Redbones	Louisiana	

NAME .... *TRIBE* .... *AREA* .... *DATE*

E

Name	Tribe	Area	Date
Eagle	Ottawa Treaty Sioux Chippewa Blackfeet Delaware Houma Fox	St. Marys, OH	1818
Eaks	Shawnee Rolls		1896
Earth	Eel River Treaty	Grouseland, IN	1805
Easter (Easterling/Easton)	 Shawnee	Mason Cty, KY Adams Cty, OH	1800 1900
Eastman	Sioux		
Eater	Creek Treaty		1814
Eaton	Cherokee Census Seminole		1835
Echohawk	Pawnee		
Eddy	Ottawa Treaty	Vincennes, IN	1805
Edenshaw	Haida		
Edgington	Delaware		
Edwards	Shawnee	Mason Cty, WV	1871
Ehyophsta	Cheyenne		
Eiselstein	Shawnee	Meigs Cty, OH	1908
Elk (Black Elk)	Wyandot Treaty Ottawa Treaty Oglala	Lake Erie St. Marys, OH	1817 1818
Elkhair	Delaware	Kansas	1867
Ellal	Pequot	Connecticut	
Elliot	Shawnee Delaware Seminole	 Muskingum Cty, OH	 1773

NAME ....*TRIBE*........................*AREA* ....*DATE*

Name	Tribe	Area	Date
Ellis	Cherokee/Shawnee Rolls		1934
El Mocho	Tonkawa		
Ely	Melungeon	NC, VA, TN, KY	
Emathala	Creek		
Emubby	Chickasaw		
End	Wyandot Treaty	Lake Erie	1817
Engler	Delaware	Oklahoma	
England	Cherokee Census		1835
English	Wyandot		
Epps	Cubans	North Carolina	
Espinosa	Miscosuhee		
Estamaza	Omaha		
Evans	Shawnee	Meigs Cty, OH	1897
	Melungeon	NC, VA, TN, KY	
Everett	Delaware	Kansas	1858
	Comanche		
Everman	Miami		
Eyes	Eel River Treaty	Vincennes, IN	1803
(Littleyes)	Wea Treaty	Grouseland, IN	1805
(Whiteyes)	Delaware Treaty	Grouseland, IN	1805
	Creek Treaty		1814
(Whiteyes)	Miami Treaty	St. Marys, OH	1818
	Wyandot Treaty	Crawford Cty, OH	1832

F

Name	Tribe	Area	Date
Face	Osage Treaty	Spring Wells	1815
	Seminole	Florida	1898
Factor	Seminole	Florida	
	Cherokee		
Fagin	Pequot	Connecticut	
(Faggin)			
Falling	Six Nations Treaty	Ft. Harmar, OH	1789
	Cherokee Census		1835

NAME............TRIBE............AREA............DATE

Name	Tribe	Area	Date
Falleaf	Delaware	Kansas	1858
Farmer(s)	Shawnee	Pike Cty, OH	1820
	Oneida Treaty	Oneida, NY	1794
	Seneca Treaty	Genesee River, NY	1802
Fast	Seneca Treaty	Lewistown, OH	1831
Fawn	Cherokee Treaty	Banks of Holston, TN	1791
	Choctaw Treaty	Hopewell, TN	1786
Fay	Seminole	Florida	
Fearon	Delaware	Oklahoma	
Feather	Delaware	Darke Cty, OH	1795
(Yellowfeather)	Shawnee	Allen Cty, OH	1817
	Six Nations Treaty	Ft. Harmar, OH	1789
	Wyandot Treaty	Greenville, OH	1795
	Cherokee Census		1835
(Yellowfeather)	Wampanoag		
Feiger	Shawnee	Meigs Cty, OH	1886
Fell	Wyandot Treaty	Lake Erie	1817
Fellow(s)	Cherokee Treaty	Banks of Holston, TN	1791
	Choctaw Treaty	Hopewell, TN	1786
	Wyandot Treaty	Spring Wells	1815
	Shawnee Rolls		1867
Ferguson	Shawnee	Wood Cty, WV	
	Delaware	Kansas	1858
Fewell	Seminole	Florida	1846
Ficklin	Seminole		
Fiddler	Delaware	Oklahoma	
Fielding	Mohegan		
Fields	Melungeon	NC, VA, TN, KY	
	Cherokee Census		1835
Filanahee	Seminole	Florida	1890
File	Delaware	Kansas	1864
Fire	Six Nations Treaty	Ft. Harmar, OH	1789
	Oneida Treaty	New York	1794
	Ottawa Treaty	Detroit, MI	1807

NAME ....*TRIBE*....................*AREA* ....*DATE*

Fire *(continued)*

NAME	TRIBE	AREA	DATE
	Chippewa Treaty	Brownstown, MI	1808
	Cherokee Census		1835
(Fire Dog)	Cheyenne		
	Lakota		
(Fire Bear)	Assiniboin		1900
Firehart	Shawnee		
First	Wyandot Treaty	Spring Wells	1815
	Ottawa Treaty	Grand River, IN	1815
	Assiniboin		1888
Fish	Delaware	Kansas	1864
	Oneida Treaty	Oneida, NY	1794
	Shawnee Rolls		1854
	Cherokee Census		1835
	Miami		
Fisher	Seneca	Sandusky Cty, OH	1817
	Cherokee Treaty		1791
	Ottawa Treaty	Spring Wells	1815
Five	Potawatomi Treaty	Ft. Wayne, IN	1803
	Osage Treaty	Spring Wells	1815
Fixico	Creek		
	Seminole		
	Shawnee		
	Sauk		
	Fox		
Flaim	Wyandot		
Fleming	Cherokee		
Fletcher	Melungeon		
	Kiowa		
Flinn	Shawnee		
Flint	Shawnee Rolls		1854
Flowers	Shawnee Rolls		1896
Fly	Chippewa Treaty	Grand River, IN	1815
Folsom	Choctaw		
	Seminole		

NAME	TRIBE	AREA	DATE
Foot	Seneca Creek Treaty Sioux Potawatomi	Sandusky Cty, OH	1817 1814
Ford	Shawnee		
Foreman	Cherokee Census		1835
Foster	Cherokee Census		1835
Fourleaf	Delaware		
Fowl	Six Nations Treaty	New York	1896
Fox	Shawnee Delaware Gnadenhutton Cherokee Treaty Wyandot Treaty	Auglaize Cty, OH Darke Cty, OH Banks of Holston, TN Greenville, OH	1817 1795 1791 1794
Fraico	Mohawk Treaty	New York	1797
Francis	Miami Treaty Shawnee Wyandot Treaty	New York City Trigg Cty, KY Sandusky Cty, OH	1790 1820 1842
Frank	Delaware Seminole	Oklahoma Florida	 1892
Franklin	Seminole	Florida	1886
Freed	Shawnee	Mason Cty, WV Washington Cty, OH	
Freeman	Melungeon		
French	Melungeon	NC, VA, TN, KY	
Frenchman	Delaware		
Friday	Yupik		
Front	Wyandot Treaty	Lake Erie	1817
Frost	Shawnee	Meigs Cty, OH	
Frozen	Shawnee Treaty	Darke Cty, OH	1814
Fulker	Wyandot		
Full	Six Nations Treaty Wyandot Treaty	Ft. Harmar, OH Lake Erie	1789 1817

NAME .... *TRIBE* .... *AREA* .... *DATE*

Name	Tribe	Area	Date
Fuller	Shawnee		
Fullerton	Shawnee	Auglaize Cty, OH	1869
Funke	Seminole	Florida	1870
Futch	Seminole	Florida	1870

G

Name	Tribe	Area	Date
Gall	Sioux		
Gann	Melungeon	NC, VA, TN, KY	
Garcia	Seminole	Florida	1816
Garden	Seminole	Florida	1840
Garland	Melungeon	NC, VA, TN, KY	
Garrett	Wyandot Pequot Cherokee	Sandusky Cty, OH Connecticut	1842
Gashwazia	Hopi		
Gates	Powhatan	Virginia	
Gay	Sioux		
Geeque	Ottawa Treaty	Darke Cty, OH	1795
Geiser	Delaware	Oklahoma	
General	Shawnee	Auglaize Cty, OH	1817
Gentleman	Cherokee Treaty	Tellico, TN	1805
George	Seneca	Sandusky Cty, OH	1817
	Delaware	Muskingum Valley, OH	1755
	Wyandot Treaty	Greenville, OH	1795
	Choctaw Treaty	Mt. Dexter	1805
	Creek Treaty		1814
	Cherokee Census		1835
	Pequot	Connecticut	
	Shawnee	Auglaize Cty, OH	1817
	Salish		
	Seminole	Florida	1893
Gerbetz	Delaware	Oklahoma	
Gerronimo	Chiricahua		

NAME	TRIBE	AREA	DATE
Gibbs	Shawnee	Meigs Cty, OH	
		Mason Cty, WV	
	Delaware	Oklahoma	
	Redbones	Louisiana	
Gibson	Melungeon	Highland Cty, OH	
		Hawkins Cty, TN	
	Shawnee	Meigs Cty, OH	
	Mingo		
	Wyandot		
Gigger	Sauk		
Giger	Sauk		
Ginger	Seminole	Florida	1896
Gipson	Melungeon	NC, VA, TN, KY	
Girtman	Seminole	Florida	1890
Girty	Six Nations	Ft. Pitt, PA	1774
	Shawnee		
	Seneca		
Giver	Creek Treaty	New York City	1790
Gladman	Delaware	Oklahoma	
Glaize	Wyandot Treaty	Greenville, OH	1794
Glass	Shawnee	Pike Cty, OH	1820
	Cherokee Treaty	Tellico, TN	1798
Glenn	Wyandot		
Glover	Choctaw Treaty	Chickasaw Bluffs	1801
Gobens	Shawnee Rolls		1896
Gochring	Delaware	Oklahoma	
God	Chippewa Treaty	Greenville, OH	1815
Godfrey	Miami	Greenville, OH	1814
	Wyandot Treaty	Forks of Wabash, IN	1842
Goen	Melungeon	Darke Cty, OH	1814
	Wyandot Treaty	Forks of Wabash, IN	1842
Going(s)	Cherokee Census		1835
	Melungeon	NC, VA, TN, KY	
	Brass Ankles	South Carolina	

NAME	TRIBE	AREA	DATE
Goins	Melungeon Brass Ankles Redbones	South Carolina Louisiana	
Gold	Cherokee		
Goldsby	Cherokee		
Gomo	Potawatomi		
Good	Creek Treaty	New York City	1790
Goodbird	Hidatsa		
Goodman	Melungeon	Hawkins Cty, TN	
Goodnight	Shawnee Rolls		1896
Goodtraveller	Delaware	Kansas	1867
Gopher	Seminole	Florida	1896
Gorden	Delaware	Oklahoma	
Gorvens	Melungeon	NC, VA, TN, KY	
Gowan	Melungeon	NC, VA, TN, KY	
Gowen	Melungeon	NC, VA, TN, KY	
Graham	Melungeon Lumbee/Croatan	NC, VA, TN, KY North & South Carolina	
Grand	Wyandot Treaty Ottawa Treaty	 Detroit, MI	1795 1807
Grant	Melungeon Wyandot		
Grass	Sauk		
Grasshopper	Oneida Treaty Cherokee Census	Oneida, NY	1794 1835
Grey (Greyeyes)	Creek Wyandot Treaty	Crawford Cty, OH	1832
Green(e)	Wyandot Pamunkey/Powhatan Shawnee	Fairfield Cty, OH Virginia	1898
Greenhorn	Comanche		
Greenwood	Cherokee Census		1835

NAME ....*TRIBE*............*AREA* ....*DATE*

Greeves	Kiowa Cheyenne		
Griffey	Delaware	Kansas	1867
Griffin	Cherokee Census Quapaw		1835
Griffith	Shawnee		
Grinter	Delaware	Kansas	
Groom	Melungeon		
Ground	Seneca Crow	Sandusky Cty, OH	1817
Grover	Seminole	Florida	1896
Guemremont	Pequot	Connecticut	
Guerrero	Ixtla	Mexico	1728
Guess	Cherokee		
Gun	Choctaw Treaty Eel River Treaty	Hopewell, TN Vincennes, IN	1786 1803
Guns	Blackfeet		
Gunter	Cherokee Census		1835
Gurge	Shawnee	Darke Cty, OH	1817
Gurst	Cherokee		
Gwinn	Melungeon	NC, VA, TN, KY	
Guy	Delaware		
Gyer	Sauk		

H

Hackley	Miami	Darke Cty, OH	1814
Hadden	Delaware	Kansas	1858
Haff	Delaware	Kansas	1858
Haggis	Delaware	Oklahoma	
Haglar	Catawba		
Hahn	Delaware	Oklahoma	

NAME	TRIBE	AREA	DATE
Hailstone	Delaware		
Hair	Miami	Darke Cty, OH	1814
(Longhair)	Seneca	Sandusky Cty, OH	1817
Haires	Melungeon		
Hairlip	Seneca	Sandusky Cty, OH	1817
Hajo	Mohawk Treaty	New York	1797
Hale	Melungeon	Hawkins Cty, TN	
Half	Oneida Treaty	New York	1794
(Halftown)	Six Nations Treaty	Ft. Harmar, OH	1789
(Halfking)	Wyandot Treaty	Lake Erie	1817
(Halfmoon)	Delaware	Kansas	1867
Hall	Melungeon	NC, VA, TN, KY	
	Seminole	Florida	1878
Hallett	Seneca		
Ham	Seminole	Florida	1870
Hamilton	Delaware	Kansas	1867
Hamor	Powhatan	Virginia	
Hammond(s)	Melungeon	NC, VA, TN, KY	
	Cherokee Census		1835
Hams	Seneca	Sandusky Cty, OH	1817
Hand	Creek Treaty		1814
Handsome	Oneida Treaty	Oneida, NY	1794
Hanewrytewa	Hopi		
Hanging	Cherokee Treaty	Banks of Holston, TN	1791
	Choctaw Treaty	Hopewell, TN	1786
Haolbrook	Potawatomi		
Haozous	Pueblo		
Harden	Shawnee	Meigs Cty, OH	1980
Hardfish	Sauk		
Hare	Ottawa		
Harlin	Cherokee Census		1835

NAME .... *TRIBE* .... *AREA* .... *DATE*

Name	Tribe	Area	Date
Harmon	Shawnee Brass Ankles Pamunkey/Powhatan	West Virginia South Carolina Virginia	
Harney	Seminole	Florida	1846
Harpole (Harpold)	Shawnee	Mason Cty, WV	1870
Harris	Seneca Delaware Lumbee/Croatan Ottawa Treaty Connecticut Catawba	Sandusky Cty, OH Kansas North & South Carolina Greenville, OH Connecticut	1817 1858 1814
Harrison	Powhatan	Virginia	
Harriss	Cherokee Census		1835
Harrot	Powhatan	Virginia	
Harry	Delaware Cherokee Census	Anadarko, OK	1876 1835
Hart	Eel River Treaty Potawatomi Shawnee	Ft. Wayne, IN	1804
Hartman	Shawnee	Ross Cty, OH	
Harvey	Lumbee/Croatan	North & South Carolina	
Harvie	Lumbee/Croatan	North & South Carolina	
Haselton	Shawnee	Meigs Cty, OH	1870
Hastings	Shawnee Rolls		1867
Hat	Wyandot Treaty	Vincennes, IN	1805
Hatcher	Melungeon		
Hatchey	Seminole	Florida	
Hatt	Delaware	Kansas	1864
Haver	Delaware	Oklahoma	
Hawk (Redhawk)	 Shawnee Delaware Cherokee Census	Muskingum Valley, OH Darke Cty, OH Kansas	1765 1777 1867 1835

NAME .... *TRIBE* .... *AREA* .... *DATE*

Name	Tribe	Area	Date
Hawk *(continued)*	Crow		
	Arikara		
	Sauk		
Hawkes	Pamunkey/Powhatan	Virginia	
Hawkins	Shawnee Rolls		1896
	Cherokee Census		1835
	Delaware	Oklahoma	
Hayes	Pima		
Haywood	Pequot	Connecticut	
	Connecticut	Connecticut	
Head	Melungeon	Highland Cty, OH	
	Six Nations Treaty	Philadelphia, PA	1794
	Cherokee Treaty	Banks of Holston, TN	1791
	Blackfeet		
	Sauk		
	Seminole	Florida	1875
Headman	Seminole	Florida	1875
Heap	Oneida Treaty	New York	1794
HeDog	Oglala		
Heel	Miami Treaty	Ft. Wayne, IN	1809
Heid	Delaware	Oklahoma	
Helderbrend (Hildrebrend)	Cherokee Census		1835
Helgeson	Delaware	Oklahoma	
Henderson	Seminole		
Hendrick(s)	Delaware	Kansas	1868
	Oneida Treaty	New York	1794
	Seneca	Sandusky Cty, OH	1817
	Melungeon	NC, VA, TN, KY	
	Cherokee Census		1835
	Mohegan		
	Mohawk		
Hendrix	Shawnee	Meigs Cty, OH	1957
	Melungeon	NC, VA, TN, KY	
	Delaware	Oklahoma	

NAME	TRIBE	AREA	DATE
Hendry	Seminole	Florida	1893
Henny	Delaware	Oklahoma	
Henry	Delaware	Ft. McIntosh	1785
	Seneca	Sandusky Cty, OH	1817
	Oneida Treaty	New York	1794
	Shawnee Treaty	Wapakoneta, OH	1831
	Wyandot Treaty	Sandusky Cty, OH	1842
	Chippewa		
Hensley	Lakota	North Dakota	
Henson	Cherokee Census		1835
	Keetoowah (Cherokee)		
Herrera	Cochite Pueblo		
Hetutchatsee	Seminole	Florida	1846
Hickery	Seneca	Sandusky Cty, OH	1817
Hicks	Wyandot	Sandusky Cty, OH	1818
		Muskingum Valley, OH	1766
	Cherokee Census		1835
Hill	Delaware	Darke Cty, OH	1795
	Seneca	Sandusky Cty, OH	1817
	Shawnee	Allen Cty, OH	1817
	Melungeon	NC, VA, TN, KY	
	Mohawk		
Hillman	Melungeon	NC, VA, TN, KY	
Hines	Delaware	Oklahoma	
Hip	Seneca	Sandusky Cty, OH	1817
Hobart	Delaware	Oklahoma	
Hocking	Delaware Treaty	Grouseland, IN	1805
Hoff	Shawnee Treaty	Vincennes, IN	1805
Hog	Cherokee Census		1835
Hogge	Pamunkey/Powhatan	Virginia	
Hogling	Shawnee		
Hogshead	Melungeon	Highland Cty, OH	
Holbrook	Wyandot		

NAME .... *TRIBE* .... *AREA* .... *DATE*

Name	Tribe	Area	Date
Holder	Cherokee Treaty	Tellico, TN	1798
Holmes	Pamunkey/Powhatan	Virginia	
Homa	Choctaw		
Home	Cherokee Treaty	Banks of Holston, TN	1791
Honas	Wyandot Treaty	St. Marys, OH	1818
Honeywell	Delaware	Kansas	1867
Hoof	Shawnee Treaty	Brownstown, MI	1808
	Wyandot Treaty	Lake Erie	1817
	Delaware Treaty	Ft. Wayne, IN	1803
	Ottawa Treaty	St. Marys, OH	1818
Hopkins	Melungeon	NC, VA, TN, KY	
Hord	Seminole		
Horn	Shawnee	Muskingum Valley, OH	1790
(Longhorn)	Delaware	Anadarko, OK	1876
(Hornet)	Cherokee Census		1835
Horse(s)	Seminole	Florida	
	Blackfeet		
	Arapaho		
	Sioux		
Hough	Seminole	Florida	1886
Houn	Seneca Treaty	Greenville, OH	1814
(Coffeehound?)			
House	Wyandot Treaty	Greenville, OH	1815
Houser	Apache		
Howe	Lumbee/Croatan	North & South Carolina	
	Sioux		
Howling	Cheyenne		
(Howling Wolf)			
Hoxie	Pequot	Connecticut	
Huffman	Delaware	Oklahoma	
Hughes	Cherokee Census		1835
	Shinnecock		
	Wampanoag		

NAME .... *TRIBE* .... *AREA* .... *DATE*

Hummingbird	Six Nations Treaty	Philadelphia, PA	1794
Humor	Creek Treaty	New York City	1790
Hun	Kickapoo Treaty		1814
Hunt	Miami	Darke Cty, OH	1814
Hunter	Seneca	Sandusky Cty, OH	1817
	Delaware	Anadarko, OK	1876
	Choctaw Treaty	Hopewell, TN	1786
	Cherokee Treaty	Banks of Holston, TN	1791
Hyatt	Redbones	Louisiana	

I

Ice	Cheyenne		
	Crow		
Indian	Creek Treaty		1814
	Osage Treaty	Spring Wells	1815
Ingraham	Seminole	Florida	1892
Iron	N. Cheyenne		
(Iron Teeth)			
Isaac	Seneca	Sandusky Cty, OH	1817
	Wyandot Treaty		1805
	Cherokee Census		1835
Inman	Shawnee	Meigs Cty, OH	1879
Ironteeth	N. Cheyenne		
Island	Seneca	Sandusky Cty, OH	1817
(Island Woman)	Cheyenne		
Ishi	Yahi Yana		
Ivey	Melungeon		

J

Jack	Miami Treaty	St. Marys, OH	1818
(Littlejack)	Delaware	Missouri	1818
	Modoc		
	Kintpuash		

NAME	TRIBE	AREA	DATE
Jacket	Oneida Treaty	New York	1795
(Bluejacket)	Wyandot Treaty	Greenville, OH	1795
	Seneca Treaty	Genesee River, NY	1802
(Bluejacket)	Shawnee	Auglaize Cty, OH	1817
Jackson	Melungeon	NC, VA, TN, KY	
	Brass Ankles	South Carolina	
Jacobs	Delaware	Muskingum Cty, OH	1755
	Onondaga		
Jake	Oneida Treaty	New York	1794
James	Redbones	Louisiana	
	Choctaw Treaty	Mt. Dexter	1805
	Miami Treaty	St. Marys, OH	1818
	Cherokee Treaty	Tellico, TN	1805
	Wyandot Treaty	Sandusky Cty, OH	1842
	Yucchi		
Jameson	Seneca		
Jancaire	Seneca		
Janitin	Kamia		
Jaques	Wyandot	Sandusky Cty, OH	1842
	Ottawa		
Jarvis	Delaware	Oklahoma	
Jass	Cherokee		
Javens	Delaware	Oklahoma	
Jaybird	Wyandot Treaty	Lake Erie	1817
Jefferson	Powhatan		
Jeffery	Cherokee Census		1835
Jemison	Seneca		1833
Jerry	Modoc		
(Humpy Jerry)			
Jewitt	Nootka		
Jim	Delaware	Kansas	1864
	Shawnee Treaty	Wapakoneta, OH	1831
	Seminole	Florida	1886

NAME	TRIBE	AREA	DATE
Joe	Seneca	Sandusky Cty, OH	1817
	Wyandot Treaty	Brownstown, MI	1808
Jolly	Cherokee Treaty	Tellico, TN	1805
John	Seneca	Sandusky Cty, OH	1817
	Cherokee Treaty	Tellico, TN	1805
	Wyandot Treaty	Greenville, OH	1814
	Ottawa Treaty	Greenville, OH	1814
	Miami Treaty	St. Marys, OH	1818
	Shawnee Treaty	Wapakoneta, OH	1831
	Choctaw Treaty	Mt. Dexter	1805
	Seminole	Florida	1893
Johnny	Shawnee	Darke Cty, OH	1777
	Seminole	Florida	1892
Johnnycake	Delaware	Darke Cty, OH	1795
Johns	Shawnee Rolls		1896
Johnson	Seneca		
	Shawnee	Meigs Cty, OH	1908
	Redbones	Louisiana	
	Lumbee/Croatan	North & South Carolina	
	Cherokee Census		1835
	Delaware	Oklahoma	
	Navajo		
	Mohawk		
	Apache		
	Shawnee		
	Delaware		
Jones	Melungeon	Hawkins Cty, TN	
	Shawnee	Muskingum Valley, OH	1772
	Delaware	Muskingum Valley, OH	1772
	Cherokee Census		1835
	Potawatomi		
	Creek		
Jose	Apache		
Joseph	Melungeon		
	Seneca	Sandusky Cty, OH	1817
	Wyandot Treaty	St. Marys, OH	1818
	Shawnee	Auglaize Cty, OH	1817
	Nez Perce		

NAME ....TRIBE............AREA ....DATE

Name	Tribe	Area	Date
Josey	Kickapoo Treaty	Greenville, OH	1795
Joshua	Delaware	Darke Cty, OH	1790s
Journeycake	Delaware	Kansas	1858
Jukes	Melungeon		
July	Cherokee		
Jumper	Seminole	Florida	
Jumping (Jumping Bear) (Jumping Bull)	Blackfoot Hunkpapa		
Junell	Delaware	Oklahoma	
Justice	Cherokee Treaty	Tellico, TN	1805

K

Name	Tribe	Area	Date
Kabotie	Hopi		
Kagmega	Potawatomi		
Kane	Delaware	Oklahoma	
Kanickhungo	Iroquois		
Kastor	Delaware	Oklahoma	
Katah	Camish		
Katlian	Tlingit		
Kawegoma	Shawnee Rolls		1896
Kearns	Shawnee	Mason Cty, WV	1840
Keaton	Cherokee/Shawnee	Morgan Cty, KY	1860
Keal (Keelswah)	Wyandot Treaty	Forks of Wabash, IN	1842
Keener	Cherokee Census		1835
Keeper	Six Nations Treaty	Ft. Harmar, OH	1789
Keer	Shawnee		
Kees	Delaware	Oklahoma	
Keiser	Shawnee	Meigs Cty, OH	1888
Keith	Melungeon	NC, VA, TN, KY	

NAME .... *TRIBE* .... *AREA* .... *DATE*

Kell	Cherokee Census		1835
Kennedy	Melungeon Guineas	West Virginia	
Kesine	Wyandot		
Ketchum	Delaware	Missouri	1818
	Miami Treaty	St. Marys, OH	1818
Kettle	Six Nations Treaty Fox	Ft. Harmar, OH	1789
Keuerleber	Delaware	Oklahoma	
Key	Oneida Treaty	New York	1794
Keyam	Plains Cree		
Killbuck	Delaware	Muskingum Valley, OH	1752
	Miami Treaty	St. Marys, OH	1818
	Osage Treaty	Spring Wells	1815
Killer	Cherokee Treaty	Banks of Holston, TN	1791
	Choctaw Treaty	Hopewell, TN	1786
	Keetoowah (Cherokee)		
Kilpatrick	Cherokee		
King	Delaware	Greenville, OH	1795
(Halfking)	Wyandot		
	Creek Treaty	New York City	1790
(Kingfisher)	Cherokee Treaty	Banks of Holston, TN	1791
	Osage Treaty	Spring Wells	1815
	Seneca Treaty	Buffalo Creek, NY	1802
	Shawnee Rolls		1854
(Little King)	Ottawa		
	Catawba		
	Matawai	Guiana	1885
Kinkhead	Delaware	Muskingum Valley, OH	1795
Kintpuas	Modoc		
Kirby	Melungeon		
Kirk	Navajo		
Kiser	Melungeon	NC, VA, TN, KY	
Kizer	Shawnee Rolls		1817

NAME .... *TRIBE* .... *AREA* .... *DATE*

NAME	TRIBE	AREA	DATE
Knause	Delaware	Oklahoma	
Knee (Stiffknee)	Delaware	Pittsburgh, PA	1788
Knife	Shawnee Treaty N. Cheyenne Wyandot	Wapakoneta, OH	1831
Knisley	Delaware	Oklahoma	
Kocaum	Powhatan	Virginia	
Koch	Comanche		
Kollman	Delaware	Oklahoma	
Koy	Delaware Treaty	Grouseland, IN	1805
Kraft	Delaware	Oklahoma	
Kreipe	Potawatomi		
Kuhn	Cherokee Treaty	Hopewell, TN	1785
Kusha	Ottawa	St. Marys, OH	1817
Kusik	Oneida Treaty	New York	1794

L

NAME	TRIBE	AREA	DATE
Labadie	Miami	Darke Cty, OH	1795
Le Belle	Shawnee	Bell Cty, KY	1816
La Boussier	Eel River Treaty	Vincennes, IN	1803
Labussier	Cherokee Sauk		
LaDemoiselle	Miami		
Ladd	Auni Winnebago		
La Chasse	Ottawa Treaty	Greenville, OH	1795
La Flesche	Omaha		
La Fontaine	Miami	Greenville, OH	1814
Lake	Oneida Treaty	New York	1794
La Malice	Ottawa	Greenville, OH	1795

NAME	TRIBE	AREA	DATE
Lance	Cherokee		
Lane	Seneca	Lewistown, OH	1831
Langevin	Pequot	Connecticut	
Langlois	Miami	Greenville, OH	1814
Langston	Pamunkey/Powhatan	Virginia	
Larkin	Cherokee Census		1835
Lasie	Lumbee/Croatan	North & South Carolina	
Last (Last Star)	Maricopa		
Laurence	Pequot	Connecticut	
Lavender	Shawnee	Mason Cty, WV	1869
Laverdure	Ojibwa		
Lawson	Melungeon	NC, VA, TN, KY	
Lax	Shawnee	Meigs Cty, OH	1888
Leader	Creek Treaty	New York City	1790
Leaf	Delaware	Kansas	1864
Leather (Leatherlips)	Wyandot Treaty		1805
Le Blanc	Ottawa Treaty	Greenville, OH	1795
Le Bold	Delaware	Oklahoma	
Le Claire	Ponca Potawatomi		
Lee	Cherokee Census Wyandot Treaty Comanche Powhatan	Ft. McIntosh	1835 1785
Leek	Seneca	Sandusky Cty, OH	1817
LeFlores	Choctaw		
Lefthanded	Navajo		
Legaic	Chinook		
Le Gault	Pequot	Connecticut	

NAME ....*TRIBE*.........................*AREA* ....*DATE*

Legs	Delaware Treaty	Grouseland, IN	1805
	Eel River Treaty	Vincennes, IN	1803
	Ottawa Treaty	Detroit, MI	1807
	Wyandot Treaty	Greenville, OH	1814
	Cherokee Treaty	Tellico, TN	1795
Le Gris	Miami	Greenville, OH	1795
Leitka	Hoh		
Le Mere	Winnebago		
Length	Oneida Treaty	New York	1794
Levi	Delaware Treaty	Grouseland, IN	1805
	Choctaw Treaty	Mt. Dexter	1805
Leviner	Melungeon		
Lewis	Shawnee	Mason Cty, WV	1868
	Wyandot Treaty	Greenville, OH	1815
	Choctaw Treaty	Mt. Dexter	1805
	Ottawa Treaty	St. Marys, OH	1818
	Seneca Treaty	Lewistown, OH	1831
	Chippewa		
Libby	Pequot	Connecticut	
Liberatore	Delaware	Oklahoma	
Librada	Cumish		
Lieutenant	Creek Treaty		1790
Lifter	Cherokee Treaty	Banks of Holston, TN	1791
Light	Assiniboin		
Lincoln	Meeskawki		
Linkin/Lenken	Shawnee	Maryland	1790
Linneas	Delaware		
Lips (Leatherlips)	Wyandot Treaty		1805
Little	Seneca Treaty	Genesee River, NY	1802
	Ottawa Treaty	Greenville, OH	1795
	Delaware Treaty	Ft. Wayne, IN	1803
	Chippewa Treaty	Brownstown, MI	1808
	Eel River Treaty	Vincennes, IN	1795

NAME .... *TRIBE* .... *AREA* .... *DATE*

Little *(continued)*			
	Miami Treaty	Greenville, OH	1809
	Wea Treaty	Grouseland, IN	1805
	Creek Treaty		1814
	Cherokee Treaty	Banks of Holston, TN	1791
	Oneida Treaty	New York	1794
(Little Chief)	Kickapoo		
(Little Wolf)	Cheyenne		
(Little Big Man)	Oglala		
	Sauk		
	Seminole	Florida	1893
Littlejohn	Cherokee Treaty	Tellico, TN	1798
Loaded	Six Nations Treaty	Ft. Harmar, OH	1789
Loamkena	Hopi		
Lock(s)	Abenaki		
	N. Cheyenne		
Lochry	Shawnee		
Locklear	Melungeon		
	Lumbee/Croatan	North & South Carolina	
Loco	Mohawk Treaty	New York	1797
Logan	Mingo	Pickaway Cty, OH	
	Shawnee		
Lollaway	Shawnee	Auglaize Cty, OH	1817
Lomaluway'ma	Hopi		
Lone	Shawnee Rolls		1896
	Blackfeet		
Long	Wyandot	Sandusky Cty, OH	1842
(Longside)	Creek Treaty	New York City	1790
	Cherokee Treaty	Banks of Holston, TN	1791
	Shawnee	Monroe Cty, OH	1821
		Greenville, OH	1795
(Longtree)	Six Nations Treaty	Ft. Harmar, OH	1789
(Longtail)	Ottawa Treaty	Grouseland, IN	1818
(Longlegs)	Delaware Treaty	Grouseland, IN	1805
	Navajo		

NAME ....*TRIBE*.......................*AREA* ....*DATE*

Name	Tribe	Area	Date
Longfellow	Cherokee Treaty	Tellico, TN	1798
	Choctaw Treaty	Hopewell, TN	1786
Longking	Creek		
Lookingglass	Modoc		
Lookout	Osage		
Loon (Whiteloon)	Miami Treaty	Greenville, OH	1795
Lootee	Seminole	Florida	1870
Lopes	Melungeon	NC, VA, TN, KY	
Lorson	Delaware	Oklahoma	
Louis	Cherokee		
Louisa	Cherokee		
Louison	Osage Treaty	Spring Wells	1815
Love	Delaware Cherokee Shawnee	Kansas	1858
Loveless	Mohawk	Muskingum Valley, OH	1788
Lowery	Cherokee		
Lowry	Melungeon Lumbee/Croatan Cherokee Census Delaware	North & South Carolina	1835
Lubbe	Choctaw Treaty	Ft. Adams	1801
Lucas/Lucus	Melungeon Lumbee/Croatan Choctaw Treaty	Highland Cty, OH North & South Carolina Mt. Dexter	1805
Ludlow	Shawnee Mingo Miami		
Lugar	Dakota		
Lusk	Shawnee		
Lutsch	Delaware	Oklahoma	
Luzern	Delaware		

NAME	*TRIBE*	*AREA*	*DATE*
Lying	Six Nations Treaty	Philadelphia, PA	1794
Lyons	Delaware Onondaga	Darke Cty, OH	1795

M

Mack	Sauk		
Maddon	Shawnee Rolls		1866
Maddox	Redbones	Louisiana	
Maggard	Melungeon	NC, VA, TN, KY	
Maggot	Seneca	Sandusky Cty, OH	1817
Mahto	Chippewa	Minnesota	
Mahwee	Pequot	Connecticut	
Major(s)	Pamunkey/Powhatan Shawnee Rolls	Virginia	1867
Male (Mail/Mahle)	Guineas Melungeon	West Virginia	
Mallet	Delaware Miami Treaty	Missouri St. Marys, OH	1818 1818
Malloney	Melungeon	NC, VA, TN, KY	
Malta	Creek Treaty	Georgia	1805
Malunthy	Shawnee		1789
Mamaday	Kiowa		
Man	Shawnee	Darke Cty, OH	1805
	Ottawa Treaty	St. Marys, OH	1818
	Six Nations Treaty	Ft. Harmar, OH	1789
	Creek Treaty	Georgia	1790
	Choctaw Treaty	Hopewell, TN	1786
	Kickapoo Treaty		1814
	Wyandot Treaty	Lake Erie	1817
	Blackfeet		
	Sioux		
	Winnebago		
	Seminole	Florida	1875

NAME..............TRIBE.........................AREA ....DATE

Name	Tribe	Area	Date
Maneater	Winnebago Cherokee		
Mangas	Mimbreno Apache		
Mann	Melungeon Delaware	Oklahoma	
Manning	Cherokee Census		1835
Manua	Keetoowah (Cherokee)		
Maquinna	Nootka		
Manucelito	Navajo		
Marked	Ottawa Treaty	St. Marys, OH	1818
Marlow	Delaware	Oklahoma	
Marrowbone	Sioux		
Marrylee	Seminole	Florida	1893
Mars	Narragansett		
Marsh	Pamunkey/Powhatan Sioux	Virginia	
Marshall	Delaware	Kansas	1858
Martinez	Taos Pueblo Navajo		
Marquette	Ottawa		
Mason	Powhatan		
Matchoquis	Potawatomi		
Martin	Shawnee Melungeon Cubans Lumbee/Croatan Cherokee Census Powhatan Wyandot	Meigs Cty, OH NC, VA, TN, KY North Carolina North & South Carolina Virginia	1938 1835
Martinez	Pueblo		
Marteller	Delaware	Oklahoma	
Mataha	Choctaw		

NAME .... *TRIBE* .... *AREA* .... *DATE*

Name	Tribe	Area	Date
Mate	Mingo		
Mathew	Wyandot Treaty	Crawford Cty, OH	1832
Matottnee	Seminole	Florida	1893
Mattaha	Delaware Treaty	Grouseland, IN	1805
Matthews	Creek Treaty	Georgia	1790
	Wyandot Treaty	Lake Erie	1817
Maurer	Delaware	Oklahoma	
Maus	Delaware	Oklahoma	
Maw	Cherokee Treaty	Georgia	1790
May	Keetoowah (Cherokee)		
Mayle	Melungeon		
	Gunieas	West Virginia	
Maytubby	Just listed "Indian"		
Means	Oglala		
Measure	Creek Treaty	Georgia	1790
Medals	Potawatomi Treaty	Ft. Wayne, IN	1809
	Osage Treaty	Spring Wells	1815
	Delaware Treaty	Grouseland, IN	1803
Medicine	Crow		
	N. Cheyenne		
Meko	Delaware	Grouseland, IN	1803
Menawa	Creek		
Mendoza	Las Casa		
Menewa	Creek		
Metea	Wyandot Treaty	Lake Erie	1817
Mexican	Navajo		
Mico	Creek Treaty	Georgia	1790
Micco	Seminole	Florida	1896
Middaugh	Delaware	Oklahoma	
Middle (Middlestriker)	Cherokee Treaty	Banks of Holston, TN	1791
Miere	Wyandot	Ft. Industry, OH	1805

NAME	TRIBE	AREA	DATE
Mike	Hualapai		
Milbourne	Shawnee Rolls		1896
Miles	Pamunkey/Powhatan	Virginia	
Miller	Delaware	Muskingum Cty, OH	
	Cherokee Census		1835
	Seminole	Florida	
Mimbres	Apache		
Minard	Guineas	West Virginia	
Miner	Melungeon	NC, VA, TN, KY	
	Guineas	West Virginia	
Ming	Delaware	Darke Cty, OH	1795
Mingo	Delaware Treaty	Grouseland, IN	1805
	Choctaw Treaty	Chickasaw Bluffs	1801
Minner	Melungeon		
Minor	Melungeon		
	Ottawa	St. Marys, OH	1817
	Guineas	West Virginia	
Misser	Creek Treaty	Georgia	1790
Mitchell	Assiniboin		
	Mohawk		
	Ojibwa		
	Ottawa		
	Mingo		
	Shawnee		
Mize	Melungeon		
Mizer	Melungeon	NC, VA, TN, KY	
Moises	Yaqui		
Molasses	Seneca	Sandusky Cty, OH	1817
Mole	Creek Treaty	Georgia	1789
	Delaware Treaty	Greenville, OH	1814
Moller	Pequot	Connecticut	
Momaday	Kiowa		
	Cherokee		

NAME............*TRIBE*............*AREA*............*DATE*

Moniac	Creek		
Monomahonga	Iowa		
Monroe	Delaware	Muskingum Cty, OH	1797
Montaya	San Juan Pueblo		
Montezuma	Yavapai		
Montgomery	Delaware Treaty	Greenville, OH	1814
Montour	Delaware	Darke Cty, OH	
	Seneca	Muskingum Cty, OH	
Moon	Six Nations Treaty	Ft. Harmar, OH	1789
	Wyandot Treaty	Lake Erie	1817
Moore	Melungeon	Hawkins Cty, TN	
	Shawnee	Meigs Cty, OH	1884
More	Cherokee Census		1835
Morgan	Navajo		
	Fox		
	Seminole	Florida	1880
Morning Star	Sioux		
Morilee	Seminole	Florida	1893
Morley	Melungeon	NC, VA, TN, KY	
Morris	Shawnee	Meigs Cty, OH	1934
Morrison	Shawnee	Meigs Cty, OH	1868
Mortine	Delaware	Oklahoma	
Morton	Delaware	Oklahoma	
Moses	Delaware	Darke Cty, OH	1795
	Wyandot Treaty	Greenville, OH	1795
	Cherokee Census		1835
	Seneca		
Mosley	Melungeon	Hawkins Cty, TN	
Mosser	Potawatomi Treaty	Ft. Wayne, IN	1805
Mother	Seminole	Florida	1875
Motley	Seminole	Florida	1853
Mounce	Cherokee	Redbird, KY	

NAME	TRIBE	AREA	DATE
Mouse	Wyandot		
Mountain	Six Nations Treaty Blackfeet	Ft. Harmar, OH	1789
Mule	Blackfeet N. Cheyenne		
Mull	Melungeon	Highland Cty, OH	
Mullins	Melungeon	Hawkins Cty, TN Highland Cty, OH	
Mountain	Blackfeet		
Mureen	Melungeon	Highland Cty, OH	
Murphy	Cherokee Census		1835
Mursh	Pamunkey/Powhatan	Virginia	
Mush	Choctaw Treaty Cherokee Treaty	Hopewell, TN Tellico, TN	1786 1805
Musketo	Wyandot Treaty	Lake Erie	1817
Muskrat	Ottawa Treaty Cherokee Census	St. Marys, OH	1818 1835
Muott	Winnebago		

Mc

McArthur	Wyandot Treaty	Greenville, OH	1815
McCalla	Seminole	Florida	
McCarty	Ottawa Treaty Chippewa Shawnee	Vincennes, IN	1805
McCleamore	Six Nations Treaty		1795
McClintock	Delaware	Oklahoma	
McCullock (McCollock)	Wyandot	Sandusky Cty, OH	1817
McCloud	Nisqualli Tulalip		
McClure	Choctaw Treaty	Ft. Adams	1801

NAME	TRIBE	AREA	DATE
McCoy	St. Francis		
McDaniel	Delaware Treaty	Greenville, OH	1814
	Cherokee Census		1835
McDonald	Osage Treaty	Spring Wells	1815
	Choctaw		
McDongal	Shawnee	Darke Cty, OH	1817
McDonnel	Seneca Treaty	Lewistown, OH	1831
McDougall	Shawnee Treaty	Wapakoneta, OH	1831
McDougal	Shawnee Reservation	Auglaize Cty, OH	1817
McElhany	Shawnee		
McErwin	Delaware	Kansas	1858
McGillivray	Choctaw Treaty	Chickasaw Bluffs	1801
	Creek		
McGillivry	Delaware Treaty	Grouseland, IN	1805
McIlvaine	Delaware	Oklahoma	
McIntosh	White Stick Creek		
McIver	Shawnee		
McKee	Shawnee		
McKeever	Wyandot		
McKemxie	Shawnee		
McKenzie	Shawnee	Meigs Cty, OH	1865
	Mingo		
McKim	Shawnee	Meigs Cty, OH	1872
McKinley	Seminole	Florida	1895
McKinney	Shawnee Rolls		1867
McLean	Wyandot	Crawford Cty, OH	1832
McLemore	Cherokee Treaty	Tellico, TN	1805
McLester	Oneida		
McNair	Shawnee	Darke Cty, OH	1817
	Cherokee Census		1835
McNamee	Shawnee	Meigs Cty, OH	1854

NAME	TRIBE	AREA	DATE
McNeal	Apache		
McNear	Shawnee Treaty	Wapakoneta, OH	1831
McPhearson	Shawnee	Lewistown, OH	1831
McQueen	Wyandot		

N

Nailor	Navajo		
Namet	Maricopa		
Nanticoke	Delaware	Missouri	1818
	Miami Treaty	St. Marys, OH	1818
Narbona	Navaho		1850
Nash	Melungeon	NC, VA, TN, KY	
Natchez	Creek Treaty	Georgia	1790
Neagey	Choctaw Treaty	Hopewell, TN	1786
	Ottawa Treaty	Ft. Harmar, OH	1789
Ned	Delaware	Anadarko, OK	1876
	Cherokee Census		1835
	Pequot	Connecticut	
Negress	Seminole	Florida	1878
Negro	Seminole	Florida	1878
Nehs/Nease	Shawnee	Meigs Cty, OH	1802
Nellie	Seminole	Florida	1893
Nelson	Redbones	Louisiana	
	Pamunkey/Powhatan	Virginia	
	Cherokee Census		1935
Neoland (Noland)	Shawnee	Muskingum Valley, OH	1765
Neptune	Passamaquaddy	Maine	
Neutral	Osage Treaty		1815
Newberry	Shawnee	Meigs Cty, OH	1869
Newcomb	Delaware	Kansas	1858

NAME .... *TRIBE* .... *AREA* .... *DATE*

NAME	TRIBE	AREA	DATE
Newcomer (Newsome)	Delaware	Muskingum Valley, OH	1770
Newland/Newlon	Shawnee		
Newell	Wyandot	Sandusky Cty, OH	1842
Newman	Shawnee Melungeon Guineas	Maryland West Virginia	1790
New(s)	Delaware Seneca	Muskingum Valley, OH Sandusky Cty, OH	1770 1817
Newport	Powhatan	Virginia	
Nez	Navajo		
Niccans	Melungeon	NC, VA, TN, KY	
Nicholas	Wyandot Oneida Treaty Melungeon Ottawa	White River, IN Sandusky Cty, OH New York Highland Cty, OH	1745 1794
Nichols	Melungeon Delaware Shawnee Cherokee	Highland Cty, OH Hawkins Cty, TN Kansas Meigs Cty, OH	1867
Nicholson	Six Nations Cherokee Census	Muskingum Valley, OH	1774 1835
Nicolet	Ottawa		
Night	Eel River Treaty	Grouseland, IN	1805
Niles	Pequot	Connecticut	
Nitsch	Seneca		
Noble	Delaware	Oklahoma	
Noel	Melungeon	NC, VA, TN, KY	
Noon	Miami	Darke Cty, OH	1814
Noonday	Shawnee Cherokee Census	Tippeconoe Cty, IN	1820 1835

NAME .... *TRIBE* .... *AREA* .... *DATE*

Name	Tribe	Area	Date
Norris	Shawnee	Maryland Meigs Cty, OH	
Nose	Seneca	Sandusky Cty, OH	1817
North (Northward)	Cherokee Treaty	Banks of Holston, TN	1791
Norwell	Kwakintl		
Nubby	Choctaw Treaty	Ft. Adams	1801
Nugent	Wyandot	Sandusky Cty, OH	1817

O

Name	Tribe	Area	Date
Oatman	Mohave		
Obeta	Nettle Carrier (Shawnee)	Overton Cty, TN	
Occum	"Wheelock's prize Indian student"		1723
Ogonse	Ottawa	Auglaize Cty, OH	1831
Ohiyesa	Santee		
Oklahombi	Choctaw		
Old (Old White Woman) (Old Bull) (Old Lady Horse) (Old Person)	 Cheyenne Sioux Kiowa Blackfeet		
Olinger	Delaware	Oklahoma	
Oliver	Shawnee	Mason Cty, WV	
Olmstead	Delaware	Oklahoma	
One	Potawatomi Treaty Ottawa Treaty	 Greenville, OH	1814 1815
Open	Oneida Treaty Creek Treaty	New York	1794 1814
Opowwum	Delaware	Anadarko, OK	1876
Oritz	San Juan		
Orontony	Wyandot	Sandusky Cty, OH White River, IN	1745

NAME .... *TRIBE* .... *AREA* .... *DATE*

NAME	TRIBE	AREA	DATE
Orr	Melungeon	NC, VA, TN, KY	
Osage	Ottawa	Auglaize Cty, OH	1831
	Creek Treaty		1814
Osborn(e)	Melungeon	NC, VA, TN, KY	
	Pamunkey/Powhatan	Virginia	
Osceola	Seminole	Florida	
	Miccosukee		
Otter	Cherokee Treaty	Banks of Holston, TN	1791
(Littleotter)	Ottawa	Darke Cty, OH	1805
	Ottawa Treaty	Detroit, MI	1807
	Kickapoo Treaty		1814
Otterlifter	Cherokee Census		1835
Ours	Shawnee	Meigs Cty, OH	
Owl	Seneca	Sandusky Cty, OH	1817
	Delaware Treaty	Grouseland, IN	1805
	Miami Treaty	Ft. Wayne, IN	1809
	Osage Treaty	Spring Wells	1815
	Creek Treaty		1814
	Cherokee Census		1835
Ox	Ottawa Treaty		1795
Oxendine	Melungeon		
	Lumbee/Croatan	North & South Carolina	

P

NAME	TRIBE	AREA	DATE
Pacan	Eel River Treaty	Ft. Wayne, IN	1809
	Osage Treaty	Spring Wells	1815
Pack	Cherokee Census		1835
Paddling	Seneca	Sandusky Cty, OH	1817
Page	Pamunkey/Powhatan	Virginia	
	Delaware	Oklahoma	
Paine	Lumbee/Croatan	North & South Carolina	
Painted	Wea Treaty	Grouseland, IN	1805
	Shawnee		
Paka	Shawnee	Bell Cty, KY	1816

NAME	TRIBE	AREA	DATE
Pamham	Pequot	Connecticut	
Panapin	Assiniboin		1850
Panthe			
Paquette	Winnebago		
Parker	Delaware	Kansas	1858
	Comanche		
	Seneca		
	Seminole	Florida	1875
Parkman	Powhatan	Virginia	
Parks	Shawnee	Auglaize Cty, OH	1817
Parsain	Potawatomi		
Parsons	Shawnee	Meigs Cty, OH	1982
Partridge	Delaware	Kansas	1864
	Potawatomi		
Pascal	Delaware	Kansas	1864
Paterson	Lumbee/Croatan	North & South Carolina	
Path	Cherokee Treaty	Tellico, TN	1805
Pathkiller	Cherokee Census		1835
Pathmaker	Assiniboin		1874
Patomoc	Powhatan	Virginia	
Patton	Delaware	Oklahoma	
Pawnee	Winnebago		
Paxinosa (Paxen/Paxenoo)	Shawnee	Muskingum Valley, OH	1762
Payne	Seminole	Florida	
Payomingo	Choctaw		
Peacock	Wyandot	Sandusky Cty, OH	1842
	Seminole	Florida	1888
Peart	Caughnewaga	Canada	1755
Pease	Crow		
Pecan	Shawnee	Miami Cty, IN	1820
	Miami Treaty	Greenville, OH	1814

NAME .... *TRIBE* .... *AREA* .... *DATE*

Name	Tribe	Area	Date
Pechaqua	Delaware	Kansas	1858
Pedagogue	Eel River Treaty	Lake Erie	1817
Peek	Shawnee		
Pemata	Shawnee	Allen Cty, OH	1817
Penn	Hoh		
Penny	Shawnee	Maryland	1790
Pepi	Shawnee	Muskingum Valley, OH	
Percy	Powhatan	Virginia	
Perish	Wyandot Treaty	Lake Erie	1817
Perkins	Shawnee	Meigs Cty, OH	
	Redbones	Louisiana	
Perrot	Ottawa		
Perry	Shawnee	Darke Cty, OH	1817
	Delaware	Kansas	1858
	Melungeon	NC, VA, TN, KY	
	Coctaw Treaty	Mt. Dexter	1805
	Wyandot Treaty	Lake Erie	1817
	Ottawa Treaty	St. Marys, OH	1818
Petalesharo	Pawnee		
Peter	Delaware	Muskingum Valley, OH	1755
	Shawnee	Auglaize Cty, OH	1831
Peters	Shawnee	Darke Cty, OH	1805
Petricola	Delaware	Oklahoma	
Pettiplace	Powhatan	Virginia	
Pettit	Shawnee	Meigs Cty, OH	
Petty	Mingo		
Phelps	Melungeon	NC, VA, TN, KY	
Phillips	Delaware	Oklahoma	
	Seminole	Florida	
Phipps	Melungeon	NC, VA, TN, KY	
Pickett	Shawnee Rolls		1896
	Cherokee		

NAME	TRIBE	AREA	DATE
Pierson	Shawnee	Meigs Cty, OH	1883
Pigeon	Ottawa Treaty	Greenville, OH	1795
Pile	Chippewa Creek Treaty	Muskingum Valley, OH	1788 1814
Pine	Creek Treaty	Georgia	1790
Pinder	Redbones	Louisiana	
Pipe	Delaware Shawnee Cherokee Census Blackfeet	Ft. Harmar, OH Walpole Island	1789 1814 1835
Pitcher	Pequot	Connecticut	
Pitchlynn	Choctaw		1820
Pissocra	Delaware	Oklahoma	
Platt	Melungeon		
Playful	Seneca	Sandusky Cty, OH	1817
Plenty (Plenty Crows) (Plenty Coups)	Cheyenne Crow		
Pleasant	Creek		
Ploughman	Eel River Treaty	Vincennes, IN	1803
Plouffe	Pequot	Connecticut	
Plume	Blackfeet		
Poey	Creek Treaty	Georgia	1796
Point	Seneca	Sandusky Cty, OH	1817
Pokagon	Potawatomi		
Pole	Shawnee	Darke Cty, OH	1777
Polinaysi	Hopi		
Pollard	Seneca Treaty	Genesee Creek, NY	1802
Polly	Melungeon	NC, VA, TN, KY	
Pontiac	Wyandot Treaty	Lake Erie	1817
Popay or Pope	Tewa Hopi		

NAME .... *TRIBE* .... *AREA* .... *DATE*

Pounds	Shawnee	Monroe Cty, OH	
Porcupine	Creek Treaty		1814
Pork	Seneca/Shawnee	Lewistown, OH	1822
Porpoise	Choctaw Treaty	Hopewell, TN	1786
Porter	Creek Shawnee Rolls Tuscaroras		1896
Potts	Powhatan	Virginia	
Powell	Lumbee/Croatan	North & South Carolina	
Powers	Melungeon	NC, VA, TN, KY	
Prantup	Oneida Treaty	New York	1794
Pratt	Delaware	Kansas	
Pretty (Pretty White Cow) (Pretty on Top)	Sioux Crow		
Price	Winnebago Delaware	Oklahoma	
Prichard	Melungeon Guineas	West Virginia	
Prince	Choctaw Treaty Cherokee Treaty Fox	Hopewell, TN Tellico, TN	1786 1798
Pritchett	Cherokee Census		1835
Proctor	Shawnee Cherokee Census	Maryland	1790 1835
Proffitt	Shawnee	Meigs Cty, OH Mason Cty, WV	
Proyer	Shawnee		
Pruitt	Cherokee/Shawnee Melungeon	Kentucky Credo, WV NC, VA, TN, KY	1880
Pucan	Potawatomi Treaty	Ft. Wayne, IN	1809
Pugh	Wyandot		

NAME	TRIBE	AREA	DATE
Pullins	Shawnee	Meigs Cty, OH	1855
Punch	Wyandot	Sandusky Cty, OH	1818
Purdy	Wyandot		
Pure	Cherokee		
Pushees	Delaware	Ft. McIntosh	1785

Q

Quake	Miami Treaty	St. Marys, OH	1818
Quaskee	Shawnee	Darke Cty, OH	1817
Quatcheebek	Pequot	Connecticut	
Queake	Delaware Treaty	Greenville, OH	1814
Queen	Cherokee Census		1835
Quick	Shawnee		
Quocheets	Pequot	Connecticut	
Quotcheath	Pequot	Connecticut	

R

Rabbit	Choctaw Treaty	Hopewell, TN	1786
	Cherokee Census		1835
Racer (Razer, Rager)	Wyandot Treaty	Greenville, OH	1795
Raccoon	Delaware	Darke Cty, OH	1795
	Osage Treaty	Spring Wells	1815
	Creek Treaty		1814
	Cherokee		
	Sauk		
Ragsdale	Cherokee Census		1835
Ramey	Melungeon	NC, VA, TN, KY	
Randall	Delaware	Kansas	1867
Rankin	Wyandot	Sandusky Cty, OH	1842
Rapport	Delaware	Oklahoma	

NAME	TRIBE	AREA	DATE
Rasnick	Melungeon	NC, VA, TN, KY	
Ratcliffe	Powhatan	Virginia	
Rattlesnake	Cherokee		
Ratliff	Cherokee Census		1835
Raughley	Shawnee		
Raush	Delaware	Oklahoma	
Rawhunt	Powhatan	Virginia	
Reasner	Delaware	Oklahoma	
Reaves	Melungeon	NC, VA, TN, KY	
Red	Cherokee Treaty	Tellico, TN	1805
	Shawnee Treaty	Greenville, OH	1795
	Oneida Treaty	New York	1794
	Seneca Treaty	Genesee Creek, NY	1802
(Red Sleeves)	Membrenos Apache		
	Sioux		
Redinger	Delaware	Oklahoma	
Reed	Wyandot	Sandusky Cty, OH	1842
	Shawnee	Mason Cty, WV	1924
	Ottawa Treaty	St. Marys, OH	1818
Reese	Cherokee Census		1835
Reeves	Melungeon	NC, VA, TN, KY	
	Chilula		
	Cherokee		
Reflection	Ottawa Treaty	Greenville, OH	1814
Reha	Miami		
Reiber	Shawnee	Meigs Cty, OH	1922
Reid	Wyandot Treaty	Greenville, OH	1815
	Haida		
Reigns	Cherokee Treaty	Banks of Holston, TN	1791
Renard	Kickapoo Treaty	Greenville, OH	1795
Renner	Delaware	Oklahoma	
Resting	Miami		

NAME .... *TRIBE* .... *AREA* .... *DATE*

Name	Tribe	Area	Date
Revels	Lumbee/Croatan	North & South Carolina	
Rice	Caughnewaga	Canada	
Richard	Wyandot Treaty	Ft. McIntosh	1785
Richardson	Pamunkey/Powhatan Haliwa-Saponi	Virginia North Carolina	
Richardville	Delaware Miami Treaty	Greenville, OH Greenville, OH	1795 1795
Richville	Delaware Treaty	Ft. Wayne, IN	1803
Ricklec	Delaware	Oklahoma	
Ridge	Cherokee Census		1835
Riegert	Sioux		
Riel	Metis	Red River	
Rigil	Shawnee		
Riley	Delaware Mingo	Oklahoma	
Rine	Shawnee	Meigs Cty, OH	
Rising	Cherokee Treaty Choctaw Treaty	Banks of Holston, TN Hopewell, TN	1791 1786
Rivarre	Miami	Greenville, OH	1814
River	Seneca	Sandusky Cty, OH	1817
Roach	Lakota Shawnee	Mason Cty, WV	1850
Roan	Shawnee Rolls		1896
Robbins	Seneca Wyandot Treaty Cherokee Census	Sandusky Cty, OH Lake Erie	1817 1817 1835
Robe	Blackfeet		
Roberson	Melungeon	NC, VA, TN, KY	
Robertaile	Wyandot	Sandusky Cty, OH	1842
Roberts	Seminole	Florida	1875
Robertson	Melungeon	NC, VA, TN, KY	

NAME .... *TRIBE* .... *AREA* .... *DATE*

Name	Tribe	Area	Date
Robin	Shawnee	Darke Cty, OH	1817
Robinson	Mingo Melungeon Ottawa Ogee	Muskingum Valley, OH NC, VA, TN, KY	1774
Rock	Sauk		
Rod	Choctaw Treaty Shawnee Rolls	Hopewell, TN	1786 1854
Roebuck	Cherokee		
Rogers	Delaware Shawnee Cherokee	Kansas Cape Girardeau Cty, MO	1858
Rolling (Rolling Thunder)	Comanche		
Romine	Shawnee		
Rose	Shawnee Crow	Meigs Cty, OH	1896
Rosebush	Blackfeet		
Ross	Cherokee Census		1835
Round	Chippewa Treaty	Greenville, OH	1815
Roush	Shawnee	Meigs Cty, OH	1858
Roughleg	Seneca	Sandusky Cty, OH	1817
Rowbideaux	Sioux		
Rowlandson	Wampanoag Narragansett		
Ruddell	Shawnee		
Rummler	Shawnee Rolls		1896
Run (Runfast)	Ottawa Treaty Seneca Treaty	Greenville, OH Lewistown, OH	1795 1831
Running	Seneca	Sandusky Cty, OH	1817
Russell	Shawnee Brass Ankles	Mason Cty, OH South Carolina	1854

NAME	TRIBE	AREA	DATE
Ruuh	Wyandot Treaty	Lake Erie	1817

$

Sacondie	Delaware	Kansas	1868
Sada	Seminole	Florida	1886
Sagamaw	Ottawa Treaty	Detroit, MI	1807
Sakee	Creek		
Salser	Shawnee	Meigs Cty, OH	1889
Salvage	Powhatan	Virginia	
Sam	Shawnee	Darke Cty, OH	1817
	Delaware	Anadarko, OK	1876
	Eel River Treaty	Grouseland, IN	1805
	Seminole	Florida	1886
Sammons	Brass Ankles	South Carolina	
Sammy	Seneca	Sandusky Cty, OH	1817
Sampson	Melungeon		
	Lumbee/Croatan	North & South Carolina	
	Pamunkey/Powhatan	Virginia	
	Cherokee		
	Creek		
Samuel	Potawatomi		
Sand	Seneca	Sandusky Cty, OH	1817
Sanders	Shawnee	Greenville, OH	1817
	Cherokee Census		1835
Sando	Jemez Pueblo		
Sandoval	Navajo		
Santank	Kiowa		
Santana	Kiowa		
Sapp	Shawnee	Meigs Cty, OH	
Sarah	Delaware	Anadarko, OK	
Sarcoxie	Delaware	Kansas	1864

NAME	TRIBE	AREA	DATE
Sassacus	Pequot	Connecticut	
Sattatha	Dogeib		
Savage	Caughnewaga	Canada	
Sawyer	Pamunkey/Powhatan	Virginia	
Sayre	Shawnee	Meigs Cty, OH	
Scattup	Pequot	Connecticut	
Schlinder	Delaware	Oklahoma	
Scordawb (Scordaub)	Pequot	Connecticut	
Schrader	Delaware	Oklahoma	
Sconchin	Muscalero		1880
Scott	Brass Ankles	South Carolina	
	Lumbee/Croatan	North & South Carolina	
	Cherokee Census		1835
	Shawnee		
Scotten	Shawnee Rolls		
Scrivener	Powhatan	Virginia	
Schwab	Delaware	Oklahoma	
Schwartz	Delaware	Oklahoma	
Seabolt	Absentee Shawnee Rolls		1934
Sears	Pequot	Connecticut	
Seattle	Duwamish	Washington	
Secaw	Ottawa	Greenville, OH	1795
Second	Creek Treaty	New York City	1790
Seed	Cherokee		
	Sauk		
Segar	Absentee Shawnee Rolls		1934
Seppline	Coeur d' Alene		
Serpent (Tattooed Serpent)	Natchez		

NAME	TRIBE	AREA	DATE
Setangya	Kiowa		
Setting	Osage Treaty		1815
Sexton	Melungeon		
Seye	Seneca Treaty	Genesee River, NY	1802
Shabonee	Ottawa Potawatomi		
Shade	Delaware Shawnee	Oklahoma	
Shaeknasty	Modoc		
Shane	Ottawa	St. Marys, OH	1817
Shanks	Shawnee	Darke Cty, OH	1795
Shannon	Shawnee		
Shaosh	Delaware		
Sharp	Choctaw Treaty Cherokee Treaty Shawnee	Hopewell, TN Tellico, TN	1786 1805
Shaw	Shawnee		
Shawnaha	Shawnee	Auglaize Cty, OH	1817
Shawnee	Delaware Cherokee Census	Kansas	1864 1835
Shawry	Cherokee Treaty	Tellico, TN	1805
Shavis	Brass Ankles	South Carolina	
She (Shi She)	Shawnee	Auglaize Cty, OH	1817
Shema	Shawnee	Auglaize Cty, OH	1817
Shenandoah	Oneida		
Shephard	Melungeon Cubans Cherokee	NC, VA, TN, KY North Carolina	
Shining (Shining Arrows)	Crow		
Shongo	Seneca		

NAME	TRIBE	AREA	DATE
Short	Melungeon Brule Sioux	NC, VA, TN, KY	
Shot (Shot Close)	Blackfoot		1826
Showry	Cherokee Treaty		1806
Shumaker	Delaware	Oklahoma	
Shyrock	Delaware	Oklahoma	
Sibila	Delaware	Oklahoma	
Sickaowie (Sickatowee/Sickawee)	Cherokee Census		1835
Side	Creek Treaty	Georgia	1790
Sides	Blackfeet		
Sight (Comes in Sight)	Cheyenne		
Signore	Seneca Wyandot Treaty	Sandusky Cty, OH Lake Erie	1817 1817
Silver	Seneca Winnebago	Sandusky Cty, OH	1817
Silverheels	Shawnee Miami Treaty	Muskingum Valley, OH Ft. Wayne, IN	1798 1809
Simmons	Yankton		
Simonds (Simons)	Pequot	Connecticut	
Sinclair	Seminole	Florida	
Singer	Creek Treaty	Georgia	1790
Sinking	Shawnee Treaty	Greenville, OH	1814
Sinte	Sioux		
Siscomb	Delaware	Darke Cty, OH	1795
Sitting (Sitting Bull)	Sioux		
Sizemore	Melungeon	NC, VA, TN, KY	

NAME .... *TRIBE* .... *AREA* ....*DATE*

NAME	TRIBE	AREA	DATE
Skeksuchs	Pequot	Connecticut	
Skidegate	Haida Wiah		
Skin (Redskin)	Delaware Treaty Seneca Creek Treaty Osage Treaty Cherokee Treaty	Grouseland, IN Sandusky Cty, OH Spring Wells Tellico, TN	1805 1817 1814 1815 1798
Skookum	Tagish		
Skush	Ottawa Treaty	Detroit, MI	1807
Sky (Skies)	Seneca Oneida Treaty	Sandusky Cty, OH New York	1817 1794
Slaughter	Melungeon		
Sleek Otter	Comanche		
Slave (Slavecatcher)	Cherokee Treaty	Banks of Holston, TN	1791
Slocum	Salish		
Slone	Delaware		
Slover	Delaware Miami Shawnee		
Small	Seminole	Florida	1890
Smallpox	Seminole	Florida	1890
Smee	Seneca	Sandusky Cty, OH	1817
Smiling	Redbones	Louisiana	
Smith	Seneca Shawnee Delaware Lumbee/Croatan Cherokee Census Caughnawaga Winnebago Powhatan	Sandusky Cty, OH Muskingum Valley, OH Meigs Cty, OH Kansas North & South Carolina Canada Virginia	1817 1755 1834 1858 1835 1755

Smith *(continued)*	Potawatomi		
	Seminole	Florida	1850
Smock	Potawatomi		
Smoke	Keetoowah (Cherokee)		
Smowhala	Wamapum		
Snagbe	Choctaw		
Snake	Shawnee	Darke Cty, OH	1817
		Muskingum Valley, OH	
	Six Nations Treaty	New York	1789
	Wyandot Treaty	Greenville, OH	1815
	Cherokee Census		1835
	Kickapoo		
Snap	Delaware Treaty	Greenville, OH	1814
Snow	Assiniboin		
	Seminole	Florida	1896
Sockum	Melungeon		
Soldier	Miami	Darke Cty, OH	1795
	Cherokee Census		1835
Solomon	Wyandot Treaty	Crawford Cty, OH	1835
Sommers	Powhatan	Virginia	
Sonsomon	Pequot	Connecticut	
Sookis	N. Cheyenne		
Soudinot	Cherokee		
Sour	Cherokee Treaty	Tellico, TN	1805
Sower	Choctaw Treaty	Detroit, MI	1807
Spangler	Potawatomi		
Spark	Ottawa Treaty	Detroit, MI	1807
Spears	Cherokee Census		1835
Speckeled (Speckeled Snake)	Cherokee		
Spelman	Powhatan	Virginia	

NAME ....*TRIBE*........................*AREA* ....*DATE*

Name	Tribe	Area	Date
Spence	Shawnee	Meigs Cty, OH	
Spencer	Cherokee Census		1835
Spicer	Seneca	Sandusky Cty, OH	1817
Spider	Sioux		
Spoon (Longspoon)	Seneca	Muskingum Cty, OH	
Spotted (Spotted Tail)	Brule		
Spring	Delaware	Oklahoma	
Sproat	Shawnee	Monroe Cty, OH	
	Delaware	Oklahoma	
Spott	Wyandot		
Spy (Spybuck)	Shawnee Treaty	Wapakoneta, OH	1831
Squaw	Seminole	Florida	1875
Stalk	Shawnee Treaty	Greenville, OH	1814
Stallard	Melungeon	NC, VA, TN, KY	
Stallion	Cherokee Treaty	Tellico, TN	1798
Stander	Delaware Treaty	Grouseland, IN	1805
Standing	Cherokee Treaty	Banks of Holston, TN	1791
	Delaware Treaty	Ft. Wayne, IN	1802
	Wyandot Treaty	Greenville, OH	1815
(Standing Rock)	Sioux		
Stands (Stands in Timber)	Cheyenne		
Stanley	Melungeon	NC, VA, TN, KY	
Starchey	Powhatan	Virginia	
Start	Winnebago Treaty	Greenville, OH	1815
Stauffer	Delaware	Oklahoma	
Steel	Melungeon	NC, VA, TN, KY	
	Blackfeet		
Steiner	Delaware	Oklahoma	

NAME..............TRIBE..............AREA..............DATE

NAME	TRIBE	AREA	DATE
Stephenson	Shawnee		
Stevens	Shawnee	Meigs Cty, OH	1918
	Lumbee/Croatan	North & South Carolina	
Stevenson	Delaware	Kansas	
Stewart	Shawnee	Greenville, OH	1817
	Pamunkey/Powhatan	NC, VA, TN, KY	
	Crow		
	Seminole	Florida	1875
Stick	Seneca	Sandusky Cty, OH	1817
	Osage Treaty	Spring Wells	1815
	Wyandot Treaty	Lake Erie	1817
Still	Cherokee Treaty	Banks of Holston, TN	1791
Sting/Stinking	Oneida Treaty	New York	1794
Stith	Powhatan	Virginia	
Stitt	Melungeon	Highland Cty, OH	
Stone	Seneca	Sandusky Cty, OH	1817
	Osage Treaty	Spring Wells	1815
(Stoneater)	Kickapoo		
(Stoneater)	Creek Treaty		1814
Stoops	Wyandot		
Storm	Cheyenne		
Stranahan	Seminole	Florida	1896
Strawberry	Fox		
Striker	Cherokee Treaty	Banks of Holston, TN	1791
Stopt	Cherokee Treaty	Banks of Holston, TN	1791
Striking	Seneca	Sandusky Cty, OH	1817
(Woman Striking)	Miami	Darke Cty, OH	1795
Strong	Blackfeet		
Strongman	Delaware	Anadarko, OK	1876
Stroud	Oneida Treaty	New York	1894
	Delaware		
Stoneeater	Miami	Darke Cty, OH	1814

NAME	TRIBE	AREA	DATE
Stookey	Wyandot Treaty	Greenville, OH	1814
Strother	Redbones	Louisiana	
Sturgeon	Cherokee Sauk		
Suddeth	Miami		
Summers	Delaware	Oklahoma	
Sun	Miami	Darke Cty, OH	1814
	Creek Treaty		1814
	Delaware Treaty	Ft. Wayne, IN	1802
(Sun Elk)	Taos		
(Sun Chief)	Hopi		
Sunrise	Creek Treaty		1814
Sunsimon	Pequot	Connecticut	
Supay	Ottawa	Auglaize Cty, OH	1817
Susain	Ottawa	Auglaize Cty, OH	1831
Sutton	Shawnee Rolls		1880
Swanuc	Delaware	Kansas	1858
Swallow	Miami Treaty	Ft. Wayne, IN	1809
Swany	Shawnee	Meigs Cty, OH	1875
Swann	Melungeon Shawnee	Maryland	1750
Sweat	Melungeon Brass Ankles Redbones	South Carolina Louisiana	
Sweet (Sweet Medicine)	Cheyenne		
Sweezy	Arapaho		1881
Swentzell	Pueblo		
Swett	Brass Ankles Pamunkey/Powhatan	South Carolina Virginia	
Swift (Swift Dog)	Melungeon Hunkpapa	Highland Cty, OH	

NAME .... TRIBE............ AREA .... DATE

Swigart	Delaware	Oklahoma	
Swimmel	Cherokee Census		1835
Swimming	Six Nations Treaty	Ft. Harmar, OH	1789
Swindall	Melungeon	NC, VA, TN, KY	
Swisher	Delaware	Kansas	1867
Sword	Seneca Lakota	Sandusky Cty, OH	1817
Symmes	Miami		
Sykes	Delaware		

ℑ

Tabbaco	Seneca	Sandusky Cty, OH	1817
	Cherokee Census		1835
Tac	Luiseno		
Tackett	Shawnee		
Tadeuskund	Delaware		
Tahoma	Navajo		
Tail	Wyandot Treaty	Lake Erie	1817
	Ottawa Treaty	St. Marys, OH	1818
Takes (Takes Paint)	Blood		
Talayesna	Hopi		
Talks (Talks Different)	Gros Ventre		
Tall	N. Cheyenne		
Tallahassee	Seminole	Florida	1890
Tallman	Seneca	Sandusky Cty, OH	1817
Tallsoldier	Blackfoot		
Tally	Cubans	North Carolina	
Taloma	Navajo		

NAME .... *TRIBE*........................*AREA* ....*DATE*

Tammy/Tamenend	Delaware		
Tanner	Wyandot	Sandusky Cty, OH	1790
	Delaware	Kansas	1867
	Ottawa		
	Ojibwa		
Tapea	Shawnee	Auglaize Cty, OH	1817
Tarbell	Caughnewaga	Canada	1755
Tarhe	Wyandot Treaty	Ft. Harmar, OH	1789
Tassel	Cherokee Treaty	Hopewell, TN	1786
Tatabem	Pequot	Connecticut	
Tate	Cherokee		
Tattooed (Arm and Serpent)	Natchez		
Taylor	Shawnee		
	Lumbee/Croatan	North & South Carolina	
	Cherokee		
Tearing	Six Nations Treaty	Ft. Harmar, OH	1789
Tecumseh	Potawatomi		
	Kickapoo		
Tekonsha	Shawnee		1820
Telle	Delaware	Oklahoma	
Ten Bears	Comanche		
Tennery	Wyandot	Sandusky Cty, OH	1842
Terrapin	Choctaw Treaty	Hopewell, TN	1786
	Cherokee Treaty	Tellico, TN	1805
Thaway	Shawnee	Auglaize Cty, OH	1817
Thebeault	Ottawa	Auglaize Cty, OH	1831
Thick	Cherokee Treaty	Banks of Holston, TN	1791
Thigh	Cherokee Treaty	Banks of Holston, TN	1791
Thom	Paiute		
Thomas	Delaware	Kansas	1858
	Seneca Treaty	Greenville, OH	1814

NAME ....TRIBE..................AREA ....DATE

Thomas *(continued)*			
	Wyandot Treaty	Lake Erie	1817
	Six Nations		
	Cherokee		
Thompson	Melungeon		
	Shawnee	Maryland	1799
	Redbones	Lake Erie	1817
	Caughnewaga	Canada	1755
	Powhatan	Virginia	
	Delaware		1776
	Cherokee		
Thorn	Shawnee		
	Potawatomi		
Thorpe	Sauk		
	Fox		
Thunder	Ottawa Treaty	Greenville, OH	1795
	Chippewa Treaty	Brownstown, MI	1808
	Ottawa Treaty	Detroit, MI	1897
	Potawatomi		
	Winnebago		
	Fox		
Thunderchild	Plains Cree		
Tiblow	Delaware	Kansas	
Tiger	Osage Treaty		1815
	Seminole	Florida	1886
Tigertail	Seminole	Florida	1870
Timberlake	Cherokee Census		1835
Tindell	Delaware	Missouri	1818
Tinker	Osage		
Tired	Eel River Treaty	Vincennes, IN	1803
Toalston	Delaware	Oklahoma	
Tobacoh	Chickasaw Treaty	Hopewell, TN	1786
Tobasco	Seminole	Florida	1860
Toddy	Navajo		

NAME ....*TRIBE*..........................*AREA* ....*DATE*

Name	Tribe	Area	Date
Tolliver	Melungeon	NC, TN, VA, KY	
Tom (Blacktom)	Wyandot Treaty Delaware Shawnee Treaty Seminole	Lake Erie Muskingum Valley, OH Wapakoneta, OH Florida	1817 1758 1831 1875
Tomahawk	Six Nations Treaty Sioux	Ft. Harmar, OH	1789
Tommie	Seminole	Florida	1880
Tommy	Shawnee Seminole	Darke Cty, OH	1817
Tony	Seminole	Florida	1880
Toonie	Cherokee Census		1835
Tooth	Creek Treaty		1814
Top	Blackfeet		
Town	Oneida Treaty Choctaw Treaty	New York Hopewell, TN	1794 1786
Trahern	Choctaw		
Trail	Shawnee	Auglaize Cty, OH	1817
Traveling	Creek Treaty		1814
Tree (Bigtree)	Six Nations Treaty Shawnee	Ft. Harmar, OH Pittsburgh, PA	1789 1788
Tripp	Wyandot		
Tsali	Cherokee		1838
Tshusick	Ojibwa		
Tuckasee	Cherokee Treaty	Tellico, TN	1805
Tucker	Cherokee Census Wyandot Seminole	Florida	1835 1870
Tun	Seminole	Florida	1890
Tunis	Delaware Miami Treaty	Missouri St. Marys, OH	1818 1818
Tupponce	Pamunkey/Powhatan	Virginia	

NAME .... *TRIBE* .... *AREA* .... *DATE*

Turkey (Turkeyfoot)	Cherokee Treaty Shawnee Treaty Potawatomi	Banks of Holston, TN Greenville, OH	1791 1814
Turley	Melungeon	Highland Cty, OH	
Turn	Chippewa Treaty	Greenville, OH	1815
Turnbull	Choctaw Treaty	Mt. Dexter	1805
Turner	Miami Melungeon Cherokee Census Delaware	Darke Cty, OH NC, VA, TN, KY Oklahoma	1814 1835
Turtle	Seneca Shawnee Delaware Treaty Cherokee Treaty Miami Treaty Blackfeet Sauk Fox Winnebago	Sandusky Cty, OH Darke Cty, OH Ft. Wayne, IN Tellico, TN Ft. Wayne, IN	1817 1795 1803 1805 1809
Turtledove	Comanche		
Turtleheart	Teton		
Tuskinagle	Mohawk Treaty	New York	1797
Twelve	Chippewa Treaty	Greenville, OH	1815
Twenty	Six Nations Treaty	Ft. Harmar, OH	1789
Twilight	Miami	Darke Cty, OH	1814
Two (Two Leggings) (Two Moons)	Oneida Treaty Crow Nez Perce	New York	1794

U

Ugly	Wyandot Treaty	Greenville, OH	1815
Underwood	Choctaw Treaty	Chickasaw Bluffs	1801
Upsetter	Cherokee Treaty	Banks of Holston, TN	1791

NAME ....*TRIBE*................................*AREA* ....*DATE*

V

NAME	TRIBE	AREA	DATE
Valdez	Kickapoo		
Van Archy	Cherokee Treaty		1835
Van Bibbler	Shawnee		
Van Cleve	Potawatomi		
Van Dunk	Melungeon		
Van Eeghen	Seneca Treaty	Genesee River, NY	1802
Vanderpool	Melungeon		
Van Guilders	Melungeon		
Van Meter	Wyandot	Land Grant	1817
	Shawnee	Meigs Cty, OH	1917
Van Metre	Wyandot		
Vann	Cherokee Treaty	Washington DC	1806
Vanover	Melungeon	NC, VA, TN, KY	
Van Staphorst	Seneca Treaty	Genesee River, NY	1802
Vantly	Shawnee Rolls		1896
Vee	Seminole	Florida	1890
Veley	Delaware	Oklahoma	
Verrazano	Powhatan		
Vespucci	Powhatan		
Vicars (Viccars/Vickers)	Lumbee/Croatan	North & South Carolina	
Victor	Kalispel		
Victorio	Mimbres		1820
Vincent (Vinson/Venson)	Huron Shawnee	Mason Cty, WV	
Voelker	Potawatomi		
Vollenhoven	Seneca Treaty	Genesee River, NY	1802

W

NAME	TRIBE	AREA	DATE
Wabashaw	Sioux		
Waldo	Powhatan		
Walford	Cherokee Census		1835
Walkara	Ute		
Waggoner	Shawnee		
Wagoh	Cherokee Census		1835
Wahcitah	Cherokee Census		1835
Waldenmyer	Delaware	Oklahoma	
Walk(s)	Wyandot Treaty	Vincennes, IN	1805
	Crow		
Walker	Cherokee Treaty		1806
	Wyandot Treaty	Spring Wells	1815
	Shawnee	Land Grant	
	Osage Treaty	Spring Wells	1815
	Ottawa Treaty	St. Marys, OH	1818
(Fast Walker)	Fox	Lake Superior	
Wallace	Delaware	Oklahoma	
	Wyandot		
Walsing	Shawnee Rolls		1896
Walter(s)	Cherokee	Lawrence & Floyd Cty, KY	1800s
	Seminole	Florida	1883
Wampey	Pequot	Connecticut	
Wangoman	Delaware	Pittstown, PA	
Wannys	Shawnee	Maryland	1790
War	Shawnee		
(Warpole)	Wyandot Treaty	Lake Erie	1817
	Miami Treaty	St. Marys, OH	1818
Warcazsanacock	Powhatan	Virginia	
Warcaziwin	Sioux		

NAME ....TRIBE........................AREA ....DATE

Name	Tribe	Area	Date
Ward	Shawnee Cherokee Treaty Seminole	Florida	1791
Ware	Redbones	Louisiana	
Warm Springs	Apache		
Warner	Shawnee	Meigs Cty, OH	1907
Warriax	Melungeon		
Warrior	Seminole	Florida	
Washburn	Melungeon Delaware	Highland Cty, OH Darke Cty, OH	1795
Wapakeche	Kickapoo		
Washakie	Shoshone		
Washington	Wyandot Delaware Shawnee	Sandusky Cty, OH Muskingum Cty, OH	1842 1794
Wasp	Six Nations Treaty	Ft. Harmar, OH	1789
Watcher	Delaware		
Water(s) (Waterhunter)	Six Nations Treaty Choctaw Treaty Wyandot Treaty Shawnee Treaty Ottawa Treaty Seneca Treaty Cherokee Census Blackfeet	Ft. Harmar, OH Hopewell, TN Vincennes, IN Greenville, OH St. Marys, OH Lewistown, OH	1789 1786 1805 1814 1818 1831 1835
Watson	Pequot	Connecticut	
Watts	Melungeon Cherokee Treaty	NC, VA, TN, KY Banks of Holston, TN	1791
Waugh	Shawnee	Scioto Cty, OH Pennsylvania Center Cty, KY	1790
Wavaka	Piaute		
Way	Oneida Treaty	New York	1794
Waylayer	Choctaw Treaty	Hopewell, TN	1786

NAME	TRIBE	AREA	DATE
Wayne	Shawnee	Darke Cty, OH	1817
Weasel (Weasel Bear)	Sioux		
Weaseca	Shawnee		
Weatherford	Creek		
Weaver	Pamunkey/Powhatan	Virginia	
Webb	Delaware Pima	Kansas	1858
Welch	Cherokee Census		1835
Weller	Delaware		
Wells	Miami	Darke Cty, OH	1814
Welsh	Delaware	Oklahoma	
Went	Ottawa Treaty	Greenville, OH	1815
Wertz	Delaware	Oklahoma	
Wesley	Cherokee		
West	Powhatan Cheyenne		
Wetzel	Shawnee		
Whatley	Pueblo		
Wheaton	Shawnee	Meigs Cty, OH	1896
Wheeler	Cherokee Census Pequot	Connecticut	1835
Whelan	Wyandot		
Whirlwind	Delaware Treaty Wyandot Treaty Cherokee Census	Greenville, OH Lake Erie	1795 1817 1835
Whip	Seminole	Florida	1880
Whiping (Whipingstick)	Wyandot Treaty	Lake Erie	1817
Whitaker	Wyandot	Land Grant	1817
White	Melungeon Pamunkey/Powhatan	NC, VA, TN, KY Virginia	

NAME ....*TRIBE*........................*AREA* ....*DATE*

White *(continued)*

NAME	TRIBE	AREA	DATE
	Lumbee/Croatan	North & South Carolina	
	Shawnee	Cape Girardeau Cty, MO	1815
	Ottawa Treaty	Greenville, OH	1795
	Osage Treaty	Spring Wells	1815
(Whiteskin)	Delaware Treaty	Grouseland, IN	1805
	Creek Treaty		1814
	Kickapoo Treaty		1814
	Seneca		
(White Frog)	Cheyenne		
(White Buffalo in the Distance)	Omaha		
	Seminole	Florida	
	Crow		
	Iowa		
	Ojibwa		
	Teton		
	Blackfoot		
	Arikara		
(White Feather)	Nez Perce		
	Winnebago		
Whited	Melungeon	NC, VA, TN, KY	
Whiteyes	Miami Treaty	St. Marys, OH	1818
	Delaware	Ft. McIntosh	1785
		Muskingum Valley, OH	1769
Whitekiller	Keetoowah (Cherokee)		
Whiteloon	Wyandot		
	Shawnee		
Whiteturkey	Delaware	Kansas	1867
Whitman	Hidasta		
	Mandan		
Whitney	Seminole	Florida	1865
Whittaker	Wyandot		
Who	Ottawa Treaty	Greenville, OH	1815
Wiffin	Powhatan		
Wilcoxen	Delaware	Kansas	

NAME ....*TRIBE*........................*AREA* ....*DATE*

Name	Tribe	Area	Date
Wildcat	Seminole	Florida	1865
Wiley	Cherokee Census		1835
Wilkins	Pamunkey/Powhatan	Virginia	
Will	Shawnee	Meigs Cty, OH Muskingum Cty, OH	
	Wyandot	Land Grant	1817
	Cherokee	Cumberland Area Muskingum Valley, OH	1773
William(s)	Choctaw Treaty	Mt. Dexter	1805
	Melungeon	Hawkins Cty, TN	
	Delaware	Muskingum Valley, OH	1773
	Pamunkey/Powhatan	Virginia	
	Brass Ankles	South Carolina	
	Wyandot Treaty	Greenville, OH	1795
	Shawnee Treaty	Wapakoneta, OH	1831
	Cherokee Census		1835
	Pequot	Connecticut	
	Mohawk		
	Oneida		
Williamson	Lumbee/Croatan	North & South Carolina	
Willie	Seminole	Florida	1865
Willink	Seneca Treaty	Genesee River, NY	1802
Willis	Redbones	Louisiana	
	Melungeon	NC, VA, TN, KY	
	Lumbee/Croatan	North & South Carolina	
Wilson	Shawnee		
	Mohawk	Muskingum Valley, OH	1788
	Delaware	Kansas	1858
	Pauite		
	Sioux		
	Cowichan		
	N. Cheyenne		
	Seminole	Florida	1875
Wiltke	Seminole	Florida	1875
Winemac	Delaware Treaty	Ft. Wayne, IN	1809
	Potawatomi		

NAME .... *TRIBE* .... *AREA* .... *DATE*

Name	Tribe	Area	Date
Winegund	Delaware		
Wingfield	Powhatan		
Winne	Powhatan		
Winnemucca	Paiute		
Wipey	Shawnee		
Wisby	Redbones	Louisiana	
Wise	Delaware Pamunkey/Powhatan Comanche	Kansas Virginia	1864
Wisecup	Melungeon	Highland Cty, OH	
Wives	Seneca	Sandusky Cty, OH	1817
Wobby	Delaware	Missouri	1818
Wold	Shawnee	Wapakoneta, OH	1817
Wolf(e)	Shawnee	Wapakoneta, OH	1817
		Meigs Cty, OH	1858
		Jackson Cty, WV	1880
	Delaware	Darke Cty, OH	1796
	Cherokee Treaty	Washington DC	1806
	Ottawa Treaty	St. Marys, OH	1818
	Creek Treaty		1814
	Ojibwa		
	Blackfeet		
	N. Cheyenne		
Woman	Blackfeet		
Womanholder	Cherokee Treaty	Tellico, TN	1789
Wood	Lumbee/Croatan	North & South Carolina	
	Six Nations Treaty	Ft. Harmar, OH	1789
	Creek Treaty		1814
Woodard	Cherokee Census		1835
Wooden (Wooden Leg)	Cheyenne		
Woods	Shawnee	Meigs Cty, OH	1833
Woolyhead	Seneca	Sandusky Cty, OH	1817

Words	Osage Treaty		1815
Worm	Cherokee Treaty	Tellico, TN	1798
Wounded	Creek Treaty		1814
Wright	Delaware Lumbee/Croatan Melungeon Comanche Choctaw	Kansas North & South Carolina NC, VA, TN, KY	1864
Wyatt	Melungeon	NC, VA, TN, KY	
Wycock (Wyouke)	Pequot	Connecticut	
Wynn	Pamunkey/Powhatan	Virginia	

℣

Yahow	Creek		
Yankee	Seneca Treaty	Lewistown, OH	1831
Yava	Tewa Hopi		
Yazz	Navajo		
Yellow (Yellowfeather) (Yellowbird) (Yellowboy) (Yellow Feather) (Yellow Hair)	Choctaw Treaty Shawnee Sioux Wyandot Treaty Seneca Wampanoag Cheyenne	Hopewell, TN Greenville, OH Greenville, OH Sandusky Cty, OH	1786 1817 1815 1817
Young	Oneida Treaty Choctaw Treaty Seneca Treaty Ottawa Treaty Cherokee Treaty Creek Treaty N. Cheyenne Shawnee Seminole	New York Hopewell, TN Genesee River, NY Vincennes, IN Washington DC Florida	1794 1786 1802 1805 1806 1814 1880

NAME	TRIBE	AREA	DATE
Yost	Shawnee	Meigs Cty, OH	1900

Z

NAME	TRIBE	AREA	DATE
Zabka	Delaware	Oklahoma	
Zambi	Palmares	Brazil	1600
Zane	Wyandot	Sandusky Cty, OH	1762
Zerkle *	Shawnee	Meigs Cty, OH	1857
Ziegler	Delaware	Kansas	1858
Zotom	Kiowa		
Zunigha	Delaware Pueblo		
Zwelling	Shawnee	Meigs Cty, OH	1940

* Note: Zerkle was changed to Circle.

NATIVE AREAS

Following is a listing of areas where First American people are known to have been. Some of these are recent, some are very old. Once into an area, usually some were left behind. You will need to place a native name in the area coupled with the time-frame.

ALABAMA
Blount County	Cherokee
Elmore County	Shawnee
Escambia County	Creek
Hale County	Talomeco
Harrison County	Shawnee
Jackson County	Melungeon, Cherokee
Mobile County	Shawnee, Creole, Cajan
Monroe County	Creole, Cajan
Montgomery County	Creek
Shelby County	Shawnee
Washington County	Creole, Cajan

ARIZONIA
Apache County	Navajo
Coconino County	Hopi, Navajo
Graham County	Apache
Navajo County	Hopi, Navajo

ARKANSAS
Benton County	Mixed Tribes
Garland County	Mixed Tribes
Hot Spring County	Mixed Tribes

Arkansas continued

Johnson County	Keetoowah Cherokee, Osage
Marion County	Shawnee
Pulaski County	Mixed Tribes
Sebastian County	Mixed Tribes
Washington County	Mixed Tribes

CALIFORNIA

Riverside County	Morongo, Cahuilla, Agua Caliente, Cabezon and Soboba Reservations

CONNECTICUT

Fairfield County	Paugussett
Litchfield County	Schaghticoke
New London County	Pequot, Narrangansett, Mohegan
Washington County	Pequot

DELAWARE

Kent County	Mixed Tribes
Sussex County	Nanticoke and Mixed Tribes

DISTRICT OF COLUMBIA

	Piscataway Indians

FLORIDA

Broward County	Seminole
Dade County	Miccosukee
Duval County	Seloy
Escambia County	Mixed Tribes
Glades County	Seminole
Hendry County	Seminole

Florida continued

St. Johns County.................Seloy

GEORGIA

Burke County ....Cherokee, Creek
Floyd County.................................Cherokee
Gilmer County................................Cherokee
Levy County ....Shawnee
Lumpkin County ....Cherokee
Murray County ....Cherokee
Muscogee County...........................Creek
Paulding County............................Cherokee
Pickens County..............................Cherokee
Pierce County ....Cherokee
Putnam County...............................Creek
Rabun County................................Cherokee
Richmond County ....Shawnee
Union County ....Cherokee
Walton County ....Cherokee
Ware County ....Creek, Shawnee there
    in 1774
Wilkinson County ....Creek

ILLINOIS

Adair County ....Sauk, Fox
Alexander County ....Mixed Tribes
Cook County ....Ottawa
De Kalb County..............................Winnebago
Fulton County................................Sauk, Fox
Gallatin County ....Shawnee
Lake County ....Shawnee, Potawatomi
La Salle County.............................Potawatomi
McHenry County............................Winnebago
Page County ....Potawatomi
Peoria County................................Mixed Tribes
Rock Island County........................Sauk
Whiteside County...........................Winnebago

INDIANA

Allen County	Ottawa
Clay County	Eel River
Daviess County	Delaware
Delaware County	Delaware, Miami
Dubois County	Delaware
Elkhart County	Delaware
Fayette County	Delaware
Fulton County	Potawatomi
Gibson County	Delaware
Hamilton County	Delaware, Miami
Knox County	Delaware
Madison County	Delaware, Miami
Marion County	Miami
Miami County	Miami
Pike County	Delaware
Randolph County	Delaware
Shelby County	Delaware
Tippecanoe County	Shawnee, Potawatomi, Miami, Ottawa, Chippewa, Kickapoo
Wabash County	Miami

IOWA

Davis County	Sauk
Des Moines County	Fox
Louisa County	Sauk, Fox
Muscatine County	Sauk, Fox
Pottawattamie County	Potawatomi
Ravalli County	Potawatomi
Tama County	Sauk, Fox

KANSAS

Franklin County	Ottawa
Johnson County	Shawnee
Wyandotte County	Wyandot

KENTUCKY

Adair County ....Cherokee, Shawnee
Bath County ....Cherokee
Bell County ....Shawnee
Boyd County ....Cherokee, Shawnee
Breathitt County ....Shawnee
Carter County ....Shawnee
Christian County ....Cherokee
Clark County ....Shawnee
Clay County......................Melungeon, Shawnee
Cumberland County ....Melungeon, Delaware
Elliott County....................Cherokee, Shawnee
Fleming County..................Shawnee
Floyd County.....................Melungeon
Franklin County.................Shawnee, Cherokee,
                 Choctaw
Grayson County.................Shawnee, Cherokee
Green County ....Shawnee
Greenup County ....Shawnee, Seneca
Hancock County.................Shawnee, Melungeon
Hopkins County..................Shawnee
Jackson County ....Melungeon
Johnson County..................Melungeon, Cherokee,
                 Shawnee
Knott County......................Melungeon, Cherokee,
                 Rappahannock
Knox County ....Choctaw, Shawnee
Lawrence County ....Cherokee, Shawnee
Leslie County ....Cherokee
Letcher County...................Melungeon
Lewis County ....Shawnee
McCreary County...............Yahoo, Shawnee,
                 Cherokee
Magoffin County................Melungeon, Shawnee,
                 Cherokee
Mason County ....Shawnee
Mercer County ....Shawnee
Monroe County ....Melungeon
Morgan County ....Shawnee, Cherokee
Muhlenberg County............Shawnee
Powell County....................Shawnee

Kentucky continued

Pulaski County	Chickamunga Cherokee
Rockcastle County	Shawnee
Rowan County	Shawnee
Russell County	Shawnee, Melungeon
Scott County	Choctaw, Seminole, Potawatomi. Many others – was the site of the Choctaw Academy – How many stayed?
Todd County	Shawnee
Trigg County	Shawnee
Wayne County	Cherokee
Whitley County	Melungeon, Cherokee, Shawnee
Wolfe County	Shawnee

LOUISIANA

Allen Parish	Coushatta, Red Bones
Avoyelles Parish	Runica-Biloxi
Calcasieu Parish	Coushatta, Attakapa
East Baton Rouge Parish	Charenton (Chitimacha)
Iberia Parish	Chitimacha
Iberville Parish	Tunica
Jefferson Davis Parish	Coushatta
Lafourche Parish	Houma
La Salle Parish	Choctaw
Martin Parish	Coushatta
Rapides Parish	Choctaw
St. Charles Parish	Chaouacha
St. Tammany Parish	Choctaw
Terrebonne Parish	Houma
Nearly every Parish in the southern portion of the state along the bayous and marshy fringes	Melungeons, Red Bones

MAINE
Aroostook County ....Malecite
Penobscot County.................................Penobscot
Washington County ....Passamaquaddy

MARYLAND
Allegany County ....Shawnee
Charles County.....................................Wesort
Dorchester County ....Nanticoke
Frederick County..................................Nanticoke
Prince George's County ....Wesort
Talbot County.......................................Shawnee, Delaware
Washington County ....Nanticoke

MASSACHUSETTS
Barnstable County ....Melungeon, Mashpee
Bristol County ....Shawnee, Mashpee
Dukes County.......................................Gay Head, Natick,
Melungeon
Norfolk County ....Mixed Tribes
Plymouth County..................................Mixed Tribes,
Wampanoag
Worcester County.................................Nipmuc

MICHIGAN
Arenac County ....Ottawa
Baraga County......................................Chippewa
Bay County...Ottawa
Cass County..Ottawa
Charlevoix County ....Ottawa
Chippewa County.................................Chippewa
Emmet County ....Ottawa
Grand Traverse County ....Chippewa
Isabella County.....................................Chippewa
Macomb County...................................Ottawa, Huron, Wyandot
Mason County ....Ottawa
Menominee County...............................Potawatomi

Michigan continued

Oakland County	Ottawa, Huron, Wyandot
Oceana County	Ottawa
Ontonagon County	Chippewa
Saginaw County	Ottawa
Tuscola County	Ottawa
Wayne County	Ottawa, Huron, Wyandot

MINNESOTA

Aitkin County	Chippewa
Beltrami County	Chippewa
Cass County	Chippewa
Cook County	Chippewa
Faribault County	Ojibwa
Goodhue County	Sioux
Koochiching County	Chippewa
Mahnomen County	Chippewa
Mille Lacs County	Chippewa
Redwood County	Sioux
Scott County	Ojibwa
St. Louis County	Chippewa
Yellow Medicine County	Sioux

MISSISSIPPI

Adams County	Natchez
Neshoba County	Choctaw

MISSOURI

Cape Girardeau County	Shawnee, Delaware
Clay County	Shawnee
Jackson County	Shawnee
Marion County	Sauk, Fox
Platte County	Shawnee

MONTANA

Big Horn County	Crow
Browning County	Blackfeet
Custer County	N. Cheyenne
Hill County	Cree, Chippewa
Lake County	Flathead
Missoula County	Blackfeet
Treasure County	Crow, N. Cheyenne
Yellowstone County	Crow

NEW HAMPSHIRE

Hillsborough County	Pennacook

NEW JERSEY

Bergen County	Melungeon
Burlington County	Delaware
Cumberland County	Melungeon
Custer County	N. Cheyenne
Essex County	Mixed Tribes
Lake County	Flathead
Monmouth County	Melungeon
Morris County	Melungeon
Passaic County	Melungeon

NEW MEXICO

Santa Fe County	Pueblo

NEW YORK

Albany County	Mixed Tribes
Allegany County	Seneca
Broome County	Nanticoke
Cattaraugus County	Seneca, Cayuga, Onondaga
Columbia County	Melungeon
Dutchess County	Mahican

New York continued

Erie County	Seneca, Cayuga, Onondaga
Franklin County	Mohawk
Genesee County	Seneca
Kings County	Mixed Tribes
Lawrence County	Mohawk
Manhattan County	Delaware, Mahican
Monroe County	Onondaga
Nassau County	Mixed Tribes
Niagara County	Tuscarora
Oneida County	Oneida
Onondaga County	Onondaga, Oneida, Cayuga
Orange County	Melungeon
Rensselaer County	Melungeon
Richmond County	Cree
Rockland County	Melungeon
Schoharie County	Melungeon
Suffolk County	Shinnecock, Setauket
Tioga County	Shawnee
Ulster County	Espous
Warren County	Abenaki
Long Island	Montauk, Poosepatuck, Setauket, Matinecock, Shinnecock

NORTH CAROLINA

Bladen County	Lumbee
Burke County	Blackhawk
Cherokee County	Cherokee
Columbus County	Lumbee
Cumberland County	Lumbee
Dare County	Machapunga
Harnett County	Lumbee
Hash County	Mixed Tribes
Haywood County	Catawba, Cherokee
Hyde County	Machapunga
Jackson County	Cherokee
Macon County	Croatans

North Carolina continued

Perquimans County	Mixed Tribes
Person County	Melungeon
Rockingham County	Mixed Tribes
Robeson County	Melungeon, Lumbee
Sampson County	Lumbee
Scotland County	Lumbee
Swain County	Cherokee
York County	Catawba

NORTH DAKOTA

Burleigh County .... Mandan

OHIO

Adams County	Shawnee
Allen County	Shawnee
Ashland County	Mohican, Delaware, Mohawk, Seneca, Mingo, Wyandot
Auglaize County	Shawnee, Ottawa, Mohawk
Brown County	Shawnee 1790
Champaign County	Shawnee, Ottawa
Clark County	Shawnee, Seneca
Clermont County	Melungeon
Columbiana County	Mingo
Coshocton County	Delaware, Caughonewaga, Mahican, Wyandot, Shawnee
Crawford County	Wyandot
Cuyahoga County	Mixed Tribes
Darke County	Shawnee, Delaware, Miami, Melungeon, Occaneechi, Wyandot
Defiance County	Shawnee
Delaware County	Wyandot, Shawnee, Delaware, Mingo
Fairfield County	Wyandot

Ohio continued

Fayette County	Melungeon, Occaneechi, Wyandot, Shawnee, Delaware, Mingo
Franklin County	Wyandot, Melungeon, Occaneechi
Gallia County	Seneca, Occaneechi
Geauga County	Occaneechi
Greene County	Shawnee, Occaneechi
Guernsey County	Delaware
Hamilton County	Mixed Tribes
Hardin County	Delaware, Wyandot
Henry County	Shawnee
Highland County	Melungeon, Wyandotte, Miami, Mingo, Delaware, Shawnee, Saponi, Occaneechi
Hocking County	Wyandot, Huron, Sandusky
Holmes County	Occaneechi
Jackson County	Occaneechi
Jefferson County	Occaneechi
Lawrence County	Shawnee, Occaneechi
Licking County	Wyandot, Shawnee, Seneca
Logan County	Seneca, Shawnee, Wyandot, Occaneechi
Lucas County	Mixed Tribes
Madison County	Wyandot
Meigs County	Shawnee
Mercer County	Miami, Wyandot, Shawnee, Delaware, Mahican
Miami County	Shawnee, Miami, Mohican
Monroe County	Shawnee
Morgan County	Munsee, Mahican
Morrow County	Occaneechi, Mahican
Muskingum County	Delaware, Shawnee, Mahican
Noble County	Shawnee, Delaware

Ohio continued

Ottawa County	Ottawa
Paulding County	Ottawa, Cherokee
Pickaway County	Mingo, Shawnee
Pike County	Shawnee, Seneca
Pleasants County	Mahican
Portage County	Mingo
Putnam County	Ottawa
Richland County	Wyandot, Shawnee, Delaware
Ross County	Shawnee, Melungeon, Wyandot, Occaneechi
Sandusky County	Wyandot, Shawnee, Seneca, Delaware
Scioto County	Shawnee, Miami, Mingo, Catawba, Seneca
Seneca County	Shawnee, Wyandot, Delaware, Seneca, Ottawa
Stark County	Wyandot, Delaware, Mahican
Summit County	Delaware, Seneca, Mingo, Wyandot, Mahican
Tuscarawas County	Delaware, Tuscarawas, Mahican
Union County	Shawnee
Van Wert County	Miami, Wyandot, Shawnee, Delaware
Vinton County	Shawnee
Washington County	Shawnee, Mahican, Delaware
Wayne County	Wyandot
Wyandot County	Wyandot

OKLAHOMA

Cherokee County	Cherokee
Oklahoma County	Shawnee
Shawnee County	Shawnee
Washington County	Delaware

PENNSYLVANIA

Allegheny County	Shawnee, Delaware, Mohican
Armstrong County	Shawnee
Beaver County	Mingo 1770, Shawnee
Bedford County	Shawnee
Berks County	Delaware, Mohawk, Shawnee
Bradford County	Mixed Tribes
Bucks County	Delaware
Burlington County	Melungeon
Chester County	Shawnee
Clinton County	Shawnee, Delaware, Pequot, Narragansett, Iroquois
Dauphin County	Shawnee, Cherokee, Mixed Tribes
Delaware County	Shawnee
Franklin County	Seneca
Greene County	Delaware, Wyandot, Shawnee, Mingo
Lancaster County	Shawnee, Iroquois, Nanticoke
Lebanon County	Shawnee
Lehigh County	Delaware
Luzerne County	Shawnee, Nanticoke
Mifflin County	Shawnee
Monroe County	Delaware
Montgomery County	Delaware
Northampton County	Shawnee, Delaware
Northumberland County	Shawnee
Philadelphia County	Delaware
Pike County	Delaware
Schuylkill County	Shawnee
Tioga County	Shawnee
Warren County	Seneca
Wayne County	Delaware
Wyoming County	Shawnee, Nanticoke, Delaware
York County	Shawnee

RHODE ISLAND

Kent County .... Narragansett
Providence County .... Narragansett
Washington County .... Narragansett, Pequot

SOUTH CAROLINA

Bamberg County .... Melungeon
Berkeley County .... Melungeon
Charleston County .... Shawnee, Melungeon
Clarendon County .... Melungeon
Colleton County .... Melungeon
Dillon County .... Lumbee
Dorchester County .... Melungeon
Marlboro County .... Lumbee
Orangeburg County .... Melungeon
Richland County .... Catawba
Sumter County .... Melungeon
Williamsburg County .... Melungeon
York County .... Catawba, Lumbee

SOUTH DAKOTA

Corson County .... Arikara
Meade County .... Cheyenne

TENNESSEE

Anderson County .... Cherokee
Bledsoe County .... Melungeon
Campbell County .... Melungeon
Cannon County .... Melungeon
Chickamauga County .... Cherokee
Claiborne County .... Melungeon
Davidson County .... Shawnee, Melungeon
Grainger County .... Melungeon
Hamilton County .... Melungeon, Cherokee,
                                                                    Shawnee
Hancock County .... Melungeon
Hawkins County .... Melungeon

Tennessee continued

Magoffin County	Melungeon
Marion County	Melungeon
McMinn County	Cherokee
Morgan County	Melungeon
Overton County	Shawnee
Rhea County	Melungeon
Roane County	Melungeon
Scott County	Cherokee
Stewart County	Melungeon
Winfield County	Melungeon

TEXAS

Bexar County	Mixed Tribes
Fort Bend County	Mixed Tribes
Harris County	Mixed Tribes
Polk County	Alabama, Coushatta
Potter County	Apache

VIRGINIA

Albemerle County	Shawnee, Occaneechi
Amelia County	Occaneechi
Amherst County	Monacan, Melungeon, Buffalo Ridge Cherokee
Brunswick County	Tutelo, Occaneechi
Caroline County	Rappahannock
Charles City County	Chickahominy
Clarke County	Shawnee
Frederick County	Shawnee, Susquehannough
Greensville County	Occaneechi
Halifax County	Occaneechi
Hampshire County	Shawnee
Hancock County	Melungeon
King and Queen County	Rappahannock
King William County	Pamunkey, Mattaponi
Lee County	Melungeon
Mecklenburg County	Occaneechi

Virginia continued

New Kent County..............................Chickahominy
Northampton County.........................Accohanoc, Accomac,
                                            Occaneechi
Orange County ....Occaneechi
Patrick County..................................Occaneechi
Pittsylvania County ....Occaneechi
Rockbridge County ....Melungeon
Scott County.....................................Melungeon
Shenandoah County ....Shawnee
Southampton County..........................Occaneechi, Nansemond
Stafford County ....Mixed Tribes, Potomac
Winchester County.............................Shawnee
Wise County......................................Melungeon
Wythe County....................................Cherokee
Tidewater area...................................Chickahominy,
                                            Rappahannock

WEST VIRGINIA

Barbour County...............................Melungeon
Berkeley County................................Tuscaroras, Shawnee
Braxton County ....Delaware, Shawnee
Clay County......................................Shawnee
Fayette County ....Shawnee
Greenbrier County.............................Shawnee
Hardy County ....Shawnee
Jackson County ....Shawnee
Jefferson County ....Shawnee
Kanawha County...............................Shawnee
Lewis County ....Delaware
Logan County....................................Shawnee
Mason County ....Shawnee
McDowell County..............................Shawnee
Nicholas County................................Shawnee
Putnam County...................................Shawnee
Randolph County ....Shawnee
Roane County....................................Shawnee
Taylor County ....Melungeon
Wood County ....Shawnee
The Canoy became Kanawhas and now live along that river.

WISCONSIN

Ashland County	Chippewa
Bayfield County	Chippewa
Brown County	Oneida
Crawford County	Winnebago
Dane County	Winnebago
Dodge County	Winnebago
Forest County	Chippewa, Potawatomi
Iron County	Chippewa
Jackson County	Winnebago
Jefferson County	Winnebago, Sauk
Kewaunee County	Winnebago
La Crosse County	Winnebago
Lee County	Melungeon
Menominee County	Menominee
Outagamie County	Oneida
Rock County	Winnebago
St. Croix County	Chippewa
Sauk County	Winnebago
Sawyer County	Chippewa
Scott County	Melungeon
Shawano County	Delaware
Vilas County	Chippewa
Walworth County	Sauk, Fox
Waukesha County	Menominee, Winnebago, Kickapoo, Sauk
Wise County	Melungeon

In Conclusion

"All well and good," you say, "but my names and places do not appear here."

Well, no matter. This is the product of only five years of study. I have really just begun. Do as I suggested. Read about the county. See what people were there.

I have come to believe that if your family has been on Turtle Island for more than 200 years, there will be a First American ancestor somewhere.

For those of you who "just feel it," I advise you to look. I have found that those people with an interest in First American history or arts and crafts usually have an unknown ancestor.

My people say that is the ancestors calling.

This book addresses only United States ancestry. Do not forget that there were and are First American people in Central and South America, as well as Canada.

I have not discussed them simply because I have not studied these areas.

The suggestions that I have given here should still be a help as you look in other areas.

HAPPY HUNTING!

BIBLIOGRAPHY

Berry, Brewton. *Almost White*. NY: Macmillan, 1963.

Bible, Jean Patterson. *Melungeons Yesterday And Today*. Jefferson City, TN: Bible, 1975.

Brandon, William. *Indians*. New York: Random House, 1963.

Cartmell, T. K. *Shenandoah Valley Pioneers And Their Descendants A History Of Frederick County, Virginia*. Bowie, MD: Heritage Books, Inc., 1989.

Catlin, George. *Letters And Notes On The North American Indians*. Avenel, NJ: Gramercy Books, 1975.

Clark, Jerry. *The Shawnee*. Lexington, KY: University Press of Kentucky, 1977.

Covington, James W. *The Seminoles Of Florida*. Gainesville, FL: University Press of Florida, 1993.

Dickinson, Johnathan. *Johnathan Dickinson's Journal*. Yale University Press: 1945.

Eckert, Alan W. *That Dark And Bloody River*. NY: Bantam Books, 1995.

Eckert, Alan W. *Twilight Of Empire*. Boston, MA: Little and Brown, 1988.

Green, Robert. *The Green Tree*. Baltimore, MD: Gateway Press, 1978.

Hauptman, Laurence M. And James D. Wherry. *The Pequots In Southern New England*. Norman, OK: University of Oklahoma Press, 1990.

Hauptman, Laurence M. *Between Two Fires: American Indians In The Civil War*. NY: Free Press Paperbacks, 1995.

Hill, George William. *History Of Ashland County, Ohio*. Cleveland, OH: Williams, 1880.

Hirshfelder, Arlene. *Native Heritage*. NY: McMillan, Inc., 1995.

Howard, James H. *Shawnee! The Ceremonialism Of A Native American Tribe And Its Cultural Background.* Athens, OH: Ohio University Press, 1981.

Jennings, Francis. *The Founders Of America.* NY: W.W. Norton and Co., 1993.

Katz, William Loren. *Black Indians: A Hidden Heritage.* NY: Aladdin Paperbacks, 1986.

Lindeman, Frank B. *Blackfeet Indians.* Avenel, NJ: Random House, 1995.

Marsh, Thelma. *Moccasin Trails To The Cross.* Upper Sandusky, OH: United Methodist Historical Society of Ohio, 1974.

Maxwell, James A, ed. *America's Fascinating Indian Heritage.* Pleasantville, NY: Readers Digest Association, Inc., 1978.

Mossiker, Francis. *Pocohontas.* NY: Da Capo Press, 1976.

Nabokov, Peter, ed. *Native American Testimony.* NY: Penguin Books, 1978.

Norris, J.E., ed. *The History Of The Lower Shenandoah Valley Counties Of Frederick, Berkeley, Jefferson And Clarke.* Chicago: A. Warner & Co., 1890.

Pangburn, Richard. *Indian Blood I.* Louisville, KY: Butler Books, 1993.

Pangburn, Richard. *Indian Blood II.* Louisville, KY: Butler Books, 1996.

Porter, Frank W. III. *The Nanticoke.* NY: Chelsea House, 1987.

Randall, Emelius O. and Daniel J. Ryan, *History Of Ohio: The Rise and Fall of an American State.* NY: Century History Company, 1912-1915.

Readers Digest Association, *Through Indian Eyes.* Pleasantville, NY: Readers Digest Association, 1995.

Tregillis, Helen Cox. *The Native Tribes Of Old Ohio.* Bowie, MD: Heritage Books, Inc., 1993.